the
handbag
to have and to hold

the
handbag
to have and to hold

Carmel Allen

CARLTON
BOOKS

THIS IS A CARLTON BOOK

Text copyright ©1999 Carmel Allen
Design and special photography copyright
© 1999, 2012 Carlton Books Limited

This edition published in 2012 by
Carlton Books Limited
20 Mortimer Street
London W1T 3JW

10 9 8 7 6 5 4 3 2 1

A CIP catalogue for this book is available from the British Library.

ISBN 978 1 84732 963 9

Printed in Dubai

Senior executive editor: Lisa Dyer
Managing art director: Lucy Coley
Designers: Barbara Zuñiga and Anna Pow
Picture researchers: Catherine Costelloe
    and Jenny Meredith
Special photography: Patrice de Villiers
Production: Janette Burgin

A Note from the Author and Publisher

Every effort has been made to include all major handbag designers, but lack of space has inevitably meant that some designers have not been included. We apologize for any omissions and hasten to add that this is in no way a reflection of the designers' ability.

CONTENTS

INTRODUCTION

I was once at a party where I happened to mention that I was writing a book about handbags. 'I have to confess', said a rather smart woman, 'that I've never carried a picture of my husband and children in my wallet, but', she continued, pulling a small well-thumbed piece of paper from her slim, velvet evening purse, 'I do carry a picture of my dream handbag.' She then showed us a picture of the Hermès Birkin as if it were her first-born. I was not at all surprised by her behaviour; when I lived in Italy I had two girlfriends who put their names down for Kelly bags at the same time so they could share the six months' wait together. It really was as if they were expecting. Some may scoff and snigger, as I did, at their mounting excitement over what is, essentially, a few pieces of leather stitched together in an artful way, but handbags are like cars – some models are vintage while others are classics, but neither is just a means of getting from A to B.

More than just a fashionable accessory, the handbag is chosen by the modern woman in the knowledge that it will become her own private but portable boudoir, office, bank and emergency kit, without which she would undoubtedly feel totally lost. Even the smallest handbag will defy the laws of physics to hold mobile phone, iPod, lipstick, mirror and hairbrush, not to mention money, credit cards, keys and the odd mint. The handbag is the lady-in-waiting to the woman who gets by without a chauffeur to drive her and a butler awaiting her arrival at home.

CHAPTER I

A HISTORY
OF HANDBAGS

AS TIMES CHANGE, SO DO HANDBAGS. I REMEMBER MY MOTHER HAVING SEVERAL SMART, SNAP-SHUT BAGS WITH SOFT SUEDE LININGS, WHICH SHE CHOSE ACCORDING TO HER SHOES, THE COLOUR OF HER SUIT AND THE OCCASION. FOR THE EVENING SHE HAD MANY OTHERS, INCLUDING SEVERAL BLACK VELVET CLUTCH BAGS OF VARYING SIZES. SHE WAS OF THE GENERATION THAT GREW UP WEARING HATS AND GLOVES, THAT WOULD NEVER DREAM OF GOING BARE-LEGGED. FOR HER, THE RIGHT HANDBAG WAS DETERMINED BY A COMBINATION OF PURPOSE AND PROPRIETY. EVEN NOW, SHE FINDS THE PAIRING OF A DELICATELY BEADED PURSE WITH TROUSERS OR AN OVERSIZED BAG WITH A FLOATY DRESS TO BE FAINTLY RIDICULOUS AND TOTALLY INAPPROPRIATE. WHEREAS FASHION ONCE DICTATED THE RULES – LIKE MATCHING HANDBAGS AND SHOES – IT NOW BREAKS THEM TO MOVE FORWARD. TOMORROW FASHION WILL CHANGE AGAIN, BUT FOR NOW WE CAN LOOK BACK AND ASSESS ALL THE CHANGES THUS FAR.

Women, it seems, have held the purse strings for a relatively short time. Although the handbag is thought of as an exclusively feminine accessory, the forerunner is the pouches men wore to carry coins in ancient times. In fact, the very words 'handbag' and 'purse' stem from the Latin *bursa* and the Greek *byrsa*, which were used to describe these small bags. Later, the Normans used an *aulmonière*, which came from the word for alms and almoner and referred to a pouch suspended from a girdle worn by men – just think of Robin Hood and the bulging bags of coins robbed from the rich and given to the poor. In the twelfth century the Italians (who else?) created the first 'designer' pouches; leather examples were made by artisans of the Florentine leather-workers guild, while elaborate silk ones were crafted in Venice. In the sixteenth century two important changes took place that enabled women to take the handbag and purse for their own. It became customary for men to give their sweethearts velvet purses containing portraits of themselves and precious keepsakes made from enamel, gems and gold. At the same time, men's clothing changed, with the introduction of wide breeches containing hidden pockets that did away with the need for purses, which had hindered weapon-carrying.

NAUGHTY NINETIES

The last ten years of the nineteenth century were affectionately known as the Naughty Nineties, a reflection of the decline of the stiff Victorian values and the rise of the *belle époque*. Those who had wealth lived extravagant lives, especially the high society in the USA, like the Stuyvesant and Vanderbilt families. Long dresses, elaborate hats and ornate, grand pieces of jewellery were the order of the day, but only for married women. It was still considered bad form for young unmarried women to encourage male attention by dressing up — status and seniority dictated one's dress code. Handbags were bejewelled, embroidered or beaded for evening, with small drawstring Dorothy bags or petite purses with wrist straps being favoured. Clutch bags and shoulder bags were not used until much later. By day, smart but very sober leather handbags were carried, similar to those used by Queen Elizabeth today. The World Fair in Paris in 1900 and the death of Queen Victoria in 1901 heralded new thinking and fresh designs. The *haut monde* and the *beau monde* were to meet. Travel remained important, not just for those working in the colonies, but also for the women who embarked on the grand tour. Luggage was essential, so companies like Louis Vuitton and Hermès flourished. Women needed hat boxes, trunks for their hooped dresses, vanity boxes for their cosmetics and travel bags that would hold everything they needed during long train or coach journeys. In 1901, Louis Vuitton created the canvas and leather steamer bag and cabin trunk, designed to fit neatly under the beds of transatlantic ships.

THE TURN OF THE CENTURY

By the beginning of the twentieth century, women were already hankering after more freedom. Travel and education meant they were no longer happy to be the passive, decorative accompaniment to a male-dominated home and workplace. In 1903 Emmeline Pankhurst founded the Women's Social and Political Union in Britain, and in doing so consolidated the suffragette movement. However, women really began to be treated differently when the First World War broke out in 1914. Their help in the war effort was necessary, and women – even those from the upper echelons of society – wanted to volunteer. Women of all classes began

mixing together and social barriers began to fall. With men at war, women took over jobs that were

traditionally in the male domain, and became train drivers, factory workers, land girls and much

more. Their clothing changed accordingly, and women began to wear dungarees, trousers, sensible

boots and scarves instead of hats. Bags became utilitarian, like game bags and cartridge bags, satchels

and despatch bags, which could be slung over a shoulder while cycling or walking to work. With

male servants at the front line and female staff working for

King and country, women who had never had to worry about

carrying their front-door key or a sandwich for lunch had to

take all they would need for the day in a heroine's handbag.

THE ROARING TWENTIES

When the war ended women were left to contemplate a new

set of rules of social etiquette. The huge number of casualties

from the war meant that there were fewer eligible men, so

unmarried women started to dress up and flirt in order to

attract a husband. Hemlines rose, hair was cut and restrictive

corsets were thrown away; the new independent woman was

a free spirit and her flapper dress reflected that. Sadly, the differences between the upper and working classes were renewed, with the socialites having a ball and the poor returning to servitude. Most people were not invited to the party that was dubbed the Roaring Twenties. For the women who were, cocktail bags were fancy affairs, elaborately beaded and embroidered. By day the clutch bag, tucked neatly under one arm, flattered the body and kept the smooth lines of the new streamlined silhouette. Travel was fashionable again, and the luxury transatlantic liners became the places to see and be seen. F Scott Fitzgerald was writing *The Great Gatsby* in the USA and Evelyn Waugh was penning *Vile Bodies* in the UK. Motion pictures started being made, Hollywood was created and glamour was everything. The jazz movement enlivened Europe and the USA and the world began to move, literally, to the sound of a new beat. In their new-found freedom, women were also beginning to play sports, especially tennis and golf, and enjoying the new experience of sunbathing on the beach. Many others took to the wheel and learnt to drive. A more active, independent life combined with more wealth meant luggage and handbags could now be luxurious as well as utilitarian.

HERMÈS KELLY

The 1930s was a time of hunger marches in the UK and the Great Depression in the USA. The world slump created an atmosphere that was not conducive to the cocktail party and even the privileged few felt the need to tame their excessive living and expensive habits. Nevertheless, the wealthy still sunbathed in the South of France and Deauville and enjoyed wearing silk pyjamas to bed. The frail economic climate can be illustrated by the fact that Coco Chanel felt it necessary to cut all her prices by half in 1932. Clothes kept the slim silhouette of the 1920s, but the waist returned. Skirts got longer and more sober in style. Handbags remained neat to lie flat against the body and in 1930 Emile Hermès included in his catalogue a 46-cm (18-inch) saddle-style bag for women (it was the original Kelly bag). At this time women were carrying their own lighter and cigarettes (without a holder), following the example set by Wallis Simpson and Coco Chanel. Women were much more independent and flaunted it by wearing trouser suits. One woman in particular, Amy Johnson, inspired many women by her brave solo flight from the UK to Australia and by the more mannish clothes she chose to wear. Despite the growing independence of women, the prevailing mood toward the end of the decade was one of austerity and anxiety, and the rise of Fascism in Italy and the Nazi movement in Germany brought about another world war in 1939.

New Look

The doom and gloom of the Second World War was alleviated by a determined effort in every social group to 'make do and mend'. Women of all classes went back to work the land and 'dig for victory', or work in the offices, factories and service industries that were bereft of men. Women could not afford, nor were they allowed, to buy new clothes. Fabric was rationed and London department stores, such as John Lewis, held fittings in basement air-raid shelters so women could try on clothes in safety and avoid the potential embarrassment of being in a state of undress should an alarm be raised. Shoulder bags were introduced at this time as part of the standard military issue.

You know it's right if it's **Vinylite** PLASTICS

- *Rich and luxurious*
- *Longer wearing*
- *Water- and mildew-proof*
- *Scuff-, craze- and weather-resistant*
- *Wash and dry like a mirror*
- *In dazzling high gloss or subtle grains and textures*

For uniform superiority of performance, choose products made of VINYLITE Brand Plastics. Because they are scientifically formulated for each specific end use, their durability is unquestionable. Look for the "Made of VINYLITE Brand Plastics" signature on the things you buy.

BAKELITE CORPORATION
Unit of Union Carbide and Carbon Corporation
30 East 42nd Street, New York 17, N. Y.

Handbag by Gem

Even though the zip had been invented by W L Judson in the 1890s, it was only now used as a fastener for bags. The shape of the cardboard gas-mask box everyone carried at all times influenced the bags of the future, with new, more three-dimensional shapes arriving later. For two decades, glamour had been the push behind fashion and accessories, but now necessity and a scarcity of materials dictated fashion and created its own style. Even when the war was over, rationing continued and spirits were understandably low. When, in February 1947, Christian Dior (backed by the textile millionaire, Marcel Boussac) showed his New Look line, which involved 14–75 metres (15–80 yards) of fabric in each outfit, women were overwhelmed by desire. The clothes were everything they could not have. One famous photograph shows a woman dressed in a three-tier swagger coat outside the Dior boutique on Avenue Montaigne, Paris. Noticeably, her bag is big, boxy and crafted from crocodile. The sheer luxury of it all could have provoked another French revolution!

Coblentz

Fifties Glamour

Europe was ready, and desperate, to show Hollywood it knew about glamour. Women were enthralled by the apparently perfect lives of the screen goddesses like Veronica Lake, Joan Crawford and later Grace Kelly, Marilyn Monroe and Ingrid Bergman. There was an understandable urge for everything to be 'happy ever after'. When the men came back from war and the economy began to pick up, women returned to the home. Those who were not either extremely rich or working class became housewives. There were new gadgets, like fridges, electric stoves, televisions, vacuum cleaners and cars, available for the growing middle classes. With all the electrical help available, there was no need for servants. For the women who did not marry, there was the opportunity of a career. The idea of a liberated sexuality was beginning to emerge with the outspoken behaviour of Brigitte Bardot. Her style was quickly

copied, like her Vichy gingham wedding dress and her small summery tote bags. The tote was ideal

for trips to the beach and shopping sprees, so housewives adopted the bag and took it, along with

a smart handbag, when shopping for groceries. Women began to carry one bag for personal

belongings and one for shopping because home delivery was on the way out.

Having closed her boutique in Rue Cambon, Paris, in 1939 when war broke out, in 1953 Coco

Chanel re-opened her couture business because sales of her scent Chanel No. 5 were dwindling.

The first shows had mixed reviews. American *Vogue* adored her modern shapes, but Europe was

still in love with the romantic New Look of Dior. When Coco Chanel showed her first quilted

bag in 1955, it became a timeless classic and the envy of every fashionable woman to date.

THE SWINGING SIXTIES

To the children of the 1950s housewife, the 1960s were an opportunity waiting to happen. Unhampered by the memories of war and rationing, they lived life to the full and were politically fearless in their actions. Nothing could tame the youngster who had grown up in a time of peace, wealth and security. The only threats were the atomic bomb, the Cold War and the repressed behaviour of their parents. The first two problems were dealt with by student protests, which demanded that the government listen to this new generation. The latter problem was countered by the young instigating a sexual revolution, facilitated by the Pill. The thigh-high, knicker-skimming miniskirt just served to state their aims: liberation from home, freedom from the shackles of a monogamous (married) relationship and equality in the workplace. Handbags changed too. Gone were the rigid, conformist shapes favoured by Jackie Kennedy, Princess Grace and the 'prim and proper'. In came the extra-long, hip-length shoulder bags made of fabric or patent leather that looked undeniably shiny and fresh to the eye. The new body shape – gangly, teenage and skinny – suited a new shape of accessory. Hipster trousers demanded low-slung belts, miniskirts looked great with boots, and skirts got even shorter with the arrival of tights. Bags, of course, looked better when they were casual and understated, or absent altogether. After all, no one who was anyone took a handbag to Woodstock.

DISCO FEVER

The 1970s were a decade of differences in fashion. The hip rock-star wedding of Mick and Bianca Jagger presented Bianca in a white trouser suit, but the stately affair of Princess Anne's marriage to Mark Phillips exhibited a high-collared, buttoned-up Susan Small dress, and Princess Caroline wore a floaty white gown when she got married to Phillipe Junot. The idealism of the young people that fed on the stability of the wealthy 1960s was to falter and turn into disillusionment and disappointment in the 1970s. The assassinations of John F Kennedy and Martin Luther King in 1963 and 1968 respectively, the student uprisings of 1968 and the Vietnam War were soon to be followed by the political scandal of Watergate and the resignation of President Nixon. Finally, the OPEC oil crisis in 1973 gave rise to an undercurrent of deep unrest. While on the surface disco fever swept through nightclubs, the anarchic feelings that led to punk rock were steadily rising. Young people began to look else-where for inspiration and they were intrigued by other cultures in the pursuit of peaceful living, thus the hippie trail – from Marrakech to India – become the fashionable thing to do. As a result of this exposure to other cultures, ethnic and so-called 'primitive' art became appreciated and was reflected in the fashions of the time. Handbags were relaxed and informal, preferably picked up on one's travels. The simple two-piece tapestry bag, stitched to a skein of twisted threads to create a shoulder strap, was a popular choice. Meanwhile, Diane Keaton as Woody Allen's Annie Hall (*see opposite*) slung an oversized bag over her shoulder, and disco divas danced around their clutch bags. Diversity was the key word for this decade.

THE POWERHOUSE EIGHTIES

With the arrival of Mrs Thatcher as the UK's first female Prime Minister in 1979, Britain entered the 1980s. After the Winter of Discontent was played out to anarchic punk music, the first steps to a spending boom were taken to

the sounds of New Romantic music. Lady Diana Spencer became a style icon with her pie-crust collars and Laura Ashley skirts, which were soon adopted as the uniform of London's Sloane Ranger. This new group of well-to-do upper middle-class Brits carried shoulder bags by Mulberry or Barbour to retain a look of the countryside – where, in theory, they owned a country pile – in the city. Women also succumbed to the Lycra revolution led by Jane Fonda. Jogging, working out and aerobic classes meant women began to carry gym bags with them, and

sportswear companies, especially Reebok and Head, captured the female market. In the workplace women were breaking through the glass ceiling to executive level – the briefcase became a mainstay and would, of course, carry a Filofax. Power dressing was the order of the day and luxury labels ruled. Versace brought sequinned glamour to the catwalks and Louis Vuitton, Hermès and Chanel captured the hearts of all logo collectors.

FULL CIRCLE

Toward the end of the 1990s the information and communication industries had taken hold and many women had a mobile phone and a Psion organizer instead of a Filofax to carry in their Prada rucksacks, as well as a laptop computer to carry in their hands. There was a backlash to the hedonism of the 1980s, brought about by the threat of AIDS and the downturn in the economy. Logos were removed or made discreet, and conspicuous spending, though still existing, was less evident. Minimalist style was just as expensive to achieve as the ostentatious look of a few years earlier. Waif-like models and grunge clothes made fashion come full circle. In the last few years of the 1990s, the fabulously expensive, unravelled and frayed Voyage dresses and cardigans, so adored by

the seriously wealthy came to epitomize the trend to appear elegantly 'down at heel' – at a price unaffordable to those who really were. Gucci enjoyed a hugely successful revival in the hands of American designer Tom Ford, who began to reintroduce logos back onto the catwalk, and soon it was cool again to have a designer bag. In response, Chanel created the first ergonomically designed handbag – the 2005 (*see below*) – which was shaped to fit the contours of the body. It was ironic that in the last year of the twentieth century, the fashion pack announced the death of the handbag as we know it. The functional 'body bag' in hi-tech, utility fabrics by directional designers such as Helmut Lang (*see right*) and Prada were a welcome change for modern women who were only too happy to let go of prim little handles and embrace the new century, hands-free and with open arms.

THE RISE OF THE 'IT' BAG

By the dawn of the twenty-first century the lust for designer handbags had grown to unprecedented heights. Thanks in no small part to the iconic television show *Sex and the City*, the latest 'it' bag had became the ultimate object of desire – not just for supermodels and celebrities, but for women from all walks of life. As the character Samantha explains in one episode about the much-coveted Hermès Birken:

'It's not so much the style, it's what carrying it means!' Women were suddenly prepared to spend more on a handbag than a holiday, and each season a new style became the only bag to be seen with, usually after appearing on the arm of the hippest star of the moment. Indeed, so intense was handbag fever and individual designs so desired, new websites sprang up offering to hire them for a fixed period for those who couldn't afford to constantly update. Designer Anya Hindmarch help kickstart the 'it' bag craze with her bespoke Be a Bag, launched at London Fashion Week in 2001. This simple tote featured your chosen photo image emblazoned across it and fast became a cult hit. And in 2005,

LEFT: VICTORIA BECKHAM, IS REPUTED TO OWN OVER 100 HERMÈS BIRKIN BAGS ALONE

OPPOSITE: TAKASHI MURAKAMI'S DESIGN FOR LOUIS VUITTON WAS A HUGE HIT IN 2003

Alexander McQueen took consumer demand to another level with the launch of his limited-edition bag, the Novak, named after Kim Novak, the iconic blonde from Hitchcock's thriller *Vertigo*. After it was announced that only 200 would be produced, the Novak became the ultimate fashion trophy, selling out before a waiting list was even compiled. But perhaps it was a 2007 advertising campaign starring Kate Moss that best summed up the mood; it featured the model lying on a beach naked except for her Longchamp handbag. The message was clear: forget clothes – it's all about the bag!

Handbags had been gradually getting larger throughout the decade, but as 2008 drew to a close, the trend for outsized designs peaked, with one study declaring that the average tote (and contents) weighed a staggering 7 pounds (3.2 kg) and warning women they were risking back problems carrying them! Fast-forward to spring 2010 and, with the country stuck in recession, everything was getting smaller and more functional again. The likes of Bottega Veneta and Alexander Wang were now designing more modest-sized bags, but with edgy embellishments such as tassels and studs. By 2011, the trend for ladylike fashion, led by royal bride Kate Middleton, heralded the comeback of the dainty clutch, as perfected by Marc Jacob. A discreet but stylish purse with just enough room for keys, a card and lipstick – a timeless item harking back to those early designs from over a hundred years before.

CHAPTER **2**

THE WHO'S
WHO OF HANDBAGS

EVERY ARTIST HAS A MUSE, SOMEONE WHO INSPIRES THEIR CREATIVE IDEAS, A WOMAN WHOSE SENSE OF SELF AND 'ESSENCE' IS POWERFUL ENOUGH TO TRANSLATE INTO AN ART FORM AND BE COMMUNICATED TO THE WHOLE WORLD. THESE CHOSEN FEW CAN BE FILM STARS, ROYALTY, SUPERMODELS OR SIMPLY SOULMATES. WHO HAS NOT DREAMT OF BEING THE INSPIRATION BEHIND A SONG, A BOOK OR A SCENT? THERE IS SOMETHING TERRIBLY ROMANTIC AND IDEALISTIC ABOUT THE WHOLE CONCEPT. HUBERT DE GIVENCHY DESIGNED CLOTHES WITH AUDREY HEPBURN IN MIND, AND CHRISTIAN DIOR CREATED HIS SCENT MISS DIOR FOR HIS SISTER CATERINE, BUT THE ULTIMATE DREAM MUSE HAS TO BE GRACE KELLY. NOT ONLY DID SHE INFLUENCE THE WORK OF FILM DIRECTOR ALFRED HITCHCOCK, SHE WAS ALSO THE INSPIRATION FOR A SCENT – FLEURISSIMO BY CREED. FOR MOST WOMEN, THOUGH, GRACE KELLY WILL BE REMEMBERED FOR THE HANDBAG THAT WAS RE-CHRISTENED IN HER HONOUR. AFTER ALL, FASHIONS MAY DATE AND SCENTS MAY FADE, BUT I HAVE YET TO FIND A WOMAN WHOSE KELLY BAG HAS LOST ITS APPEAL.

F or a bag to achieve cult status it needs to be totally and utterly desirable. Of course, this is determined in part by its design, quality and charm, but a breathtakingly high price tag and a long waiting list make it all the more covetable. However, for a handbag to go down in history as a cult item, it must also be seen on the arms of the world's most fashionable, beautiful and famous women.

HANDBAGS FROM FICTION

For many, the earliest memory of a handbag is Mary Poppins' carpet bag. When P L Travers wrote his children's story about the magical English nanny who arrives on the east wind, he gave her a Gladstone bag from which she pulled all sorts of weird and wonderful things, to the utmost surprise of her charges. If the character had been male, he would have pulled his props from a black top hat in true magician style, but for a woman, a handbag was much more appropriate. The scene in the book also reinforced the idea that women carry everything but the kitchen sink in their handbags.

Another literary handbag that no young school child forgets is the one found in Oscar Wilde's *The Importance of Being Earnest*. When the snobbish

ABOVE: **A MULBERRY BAG, REMINISCENT OF MARY POPPINS' CARPET BAG**

Lady Bracknell is checking up on the family connections of Jack Worthing, who wishes to marry her daughter Gwendolen, she is horrified to find he has lost both parents. He explains to her that, in fact, they lost him, and he was found at Victoria Station in a handbag. 'A hand-bag?' she asks. 'Yes Lady Bracknell,' replies Jack. 'I was in a hand-bag — a somewhat large, black leather hand-bag, with handles to it — an ordinary hand-bag in fact.' The scene was immortalized by Edith Evans as Lady Bracknell in Anthony Asquith's elegant adaptation of the play for the cinema in 1952. Evans's incredulous look when she shrieks 'A hand-bag?' is indelibly cast in the minds of all who have seen it.

In the 1990s, small children were more likely to be familiar with the handbag collection of Tinky Winky, one of the cuddly characters in the hugely successful TV programme, *Teletubbies*. When the show was launched in France, Tinky Winky's handbag-carrying caused much consternation among parents who were worried that this feminine behaviour might influence their own offspring and encourage homosexual tendencies.

ABOVE: 'IS THIS THE HANDBAG, MISS PRISM? EXAMINE IT CAREFULLY BEFORE YOU SPEAK.' MICHAEL REDGRAVE AND MARGARET RUTHERFORD IN *THE IMPORTANCE OF BEING EARNEST*

THE FASHION INTELLIGENTSIA

During the 1950s, Diana Vreeland, editor-in-chief of American *Vogue* and contemporary of Wallis Simpson, announced to her bemused magazine staff, 'We are going to eliminate all handbags'. The adoption of male-style clothing, with all its practical pockets, would make it easier for women to leave their handbags at home, but what Vreeland had not considered was the fact that

women actually liked to carry bags. It was *Vogue* that wrote about the 'multiplicity of pockets' on Coco Chanel's suits, with 'real pockets made to hold a key, a lighter, whatever', but when Coco Chanel created her quilted bag with gilt chain straps in 1955, Diana Vreeland was among the first to snap one up.

For New York hairstylist Frédéric Fekkai, handbags were such an obsession that he created his own collection. Amazed at the variety of handbags carried by his clients, who included some of the fashion world's most influential and stylish women, and after

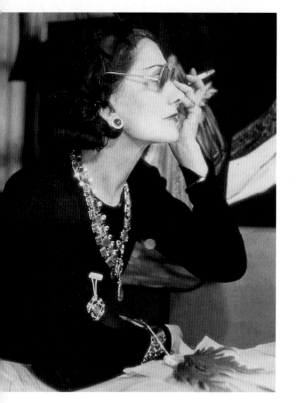

LEFT: COCO CHANEL
ABOVE: DIANA VREELAND WITH THE ONE-SEAM COAT BY BALENCIAGA

LEFT: THE DUKE AND DUCHESS OF WINDSOR STEP OUT. NOTICE THE INSIGNIA (*RIGHT*) ON HER CROCODILE BAG – TWO WS, FOR WINDSOR AND WALLIS, ENTWINED BENEATH A CROWN

months of seeing what styles worked and what did not, he decided to create his own range that placed function as high as form on the design agenda.

Kate Spade, who was accessories editor on *Mademoiselle* magazine in the USA, had similar reasons for launching her own completely new range of handbags. Like Frédéric Fekkai, her position made her privy to insider information that made her acutely aware of what women wanted from their handbags, so she set out to provide it for them. The success of her company shows that she got it right and managed to fulfil the criteria.

REGAL MUSES

Although public figures naturally have the attention of the world at large, there are only a handful that carry it well, with refinement and respectability. Grace Kelly was one who inspired women with her timeless, pared-down elegance. In 1956 she made the front cover of *Life* magazine in a photograph showing her holding her Hermès *petit sac haut à courroies* in front of her body to shield her pregnant stomach from the glare of the cameras. Although Hermès had already renamed the bag 'the Kelly' in 1955 to mark her wedding to Prince Rainier of Monaco, because Grace had carried one throughout most of her engagement, nothing quite prepared them for the effect this cover picture was to have, and there has been a six months' waiting list for a Kelly bag ever since. Not surprisingly, Princess Caroline of Monaco, their first daughter, has become a style icon in her own right and still carries the Kelly bag so favoured by her mother.

Jackie Kennedy, along with her husband, was famously acknowledged as 'American royalty' and she conveyed a sense of perfect decorum and chic style

LEFT: JACKIE KENNEDY IN LONDON
OPPOSITE: GRACE KELLY ARRIVES AT HER PARENTS' HOME FOLLOWING HER ENGAGEMENT TO PRINCE RAINIER   *ABOVE RIGHT:* THEIR FIRST DAUGHTER, CAROLINE

that was admired worldwide. Every handbag, suit and dress she wore was copied for the crowds of American women infatuated by their First Lady's sense of style and the casual effortlessness with which she carried off even the most 'dressy' outfits. Throughout her life she was photographed by the paparazzi, so her vast collection of handbags have been well documented, and women have been able to imitate her style easily, if not always successfully.

The most beloved member of royalty in the 1990s was of course Diana, Princess of Wales. The Lady Dior handbag, with its gold letter charms spelling out D. I. O. R. dangling from the handle, would always have been a best-seller, no doubt, but when Diana started to carry one, the rest of the world's well-dressed — and well-highlighted — women wanted one too. In the twenty-first century, it is now the Duchess of Cambridge who is watched by all as she carries her Mulberry Polly Push Lock tote or J P Tod's D-Bag.

RIGHT: THE LADY DIOR HANDBAG WITH ITS GOLD LETTER CHARMS SPELLING OUT D. I. O. R., WORN BY PRINCESS DIANA

THE ACTRESS AND THE HANDBAG

Many column inches in women's magazines have been devoted to actresses and their

choice of handbags, though few famous women have had a direct influence on the

design of a bag. In 1984 the actress and model Jane Birkin found herself sitting next to

Hermès's President Jean-Louis Dumas aboard an airline flight. He saw she was struggling

with a large straw tote bag, filled with all the paraphernalia she

needed to carry for her small daughter Charlotte.

While they travelled, they started to design a bag

that would be easy to open and capacious enough to

hold everything a young mother might need. The Birkin

bag – and another cult must-have – was born.

Catherine Deneuve, the French ex-Chanel model

and actress, also shares the honour of having her

LEFT TO RIGHT: ACTRESS
JANE BIRKIN; THE BIRKIN
BAG BY HERMÈS; ACTRESS
CATHERINE DENEUVE

name given to a handbag. The Catherine Deneuve bag by Fendi was designed so Catherine could keep her purse and make-up in the top part, while a secret bottom case held documents or jewellery safely locked away.

The trend for fashion magazines to forgo models on their covers in favour of celebrities shows just how much actresses and singers can influence our purchases. When American *Vogue* knows it can sell more copies with a picture of Michelle Obama on the cover rather than Heidi Klum, you can be sure that a picture of Mary-Kate Olsen or Jennifer Aniston carrying a particular handbag or wearing a particular dress will have a massive effect on the sale of those items. In fact, it's now actresses more than models who are advertising handbags, with Madonna being signed to Louis Vuitton in 2009 and Gwyneth Paltrow becoming the face for Coach in 2011.

FAR LEFT: **ACTRESS GWYNETH PALTROW**
LEFT: **ACTRESS JENNIFER LOPEZ**
ABOVE: **MADONNA**

STYLE SHAPERS AND SUPERMODELS

Although some companies refuse to say who their famous customers are, there can be no denying the fact that they reap the benefits when newspapers and magazines show pictures of their clients carrying their handbags. The interest generated from the picture of the model and television presenter Alexa Chung carrying a Mulberry bag is far greater than any amount of carefully placed advertising; in fact, newspaper headlines declared that Mulberry profits rocketed 38 per cent in 2010 thanks to the celebrity-inspired Alexa satchel.

The clothes and bags female celebrities choose to wear make a huge impact on fashion for ordinary women. In the 1980s, not one film premiere nor one fashion show was attended without a slew of Chanel bags being seen and photographed, but by the end of the decade Prada had replaced Chanel. In the 1990s it may have been the Lady Dior or the Fendi Baguette but then the boho-chic Chloé Paddington and Marc Jacob's quilted Stam were big-hitters of the new millennium.

RIGHT: ALEXA CHUNG WITH A MINI VERSION OF THE ALEXA MULBERRY BAG NAMED AFTER HER

CHAPTER **3**

BAGS OF STYLE

THE FREUDIANS WERE THE FIRST TO SEE HANDBAGS AS A SEXUAL INDICATOR, FOLLOWING ON FROM THE EARLY SEVENTEENTH-CENTURY USE OF THE WORD 'PURSE' TO INDICATE FEMALE PUDENDA. CERTAINLY NO WOMAN WANTS TO BE CALLED AN OLD BAG, BUT REVERSE CHIC WOULD ENCOURAGE THE YOUNG AND HIP TO SCOUR FLEA MARKETS FOR EXACTLY THAT ITEM. SO WHAT DOES YOUR CHOICE OF BAG SAY ABOUT YOUR PERSONALITY? ARE YOU AUTHORITATIVE? A STURDY, SAFE HANDBAG. ARE YOU VERSATILE AND SPONTANEOUS? A BACKPACK. ARE YOU OPEN AND ACCESSIBLE? A TOTE BAG. ARE YOU STATUS-CONSCIOUS? A DESIGNER BAG. ALL WILL BE REVEALED . . .

What does your choice of handbag say about you? Do the items you carry within it consolidate your outer image? We are all quick to presume the contents of a bag by its outward appearance, and quite often we feel able to judge the character of the person who is carrying it, too.

A SYMBOL OF POWER

The press attention given to the handbag of the former Prime Minister Mrs Thatcher (*see left*) is an excellent example. 'That shiny black handbag is as lethal as ever,' ran the *Sun* newspaper. In *The Times,* June 1982, Julian Critchley wrote: 'She has been beastly to the Bank of England, has demanded that the BBC "set its house in order" and tends to believe the worst of the Foreign and Commonwealth Office. She cannot see an institution without hitting it with her handbag.' 'It represented female power – an assertive woman's determination to impose her will on men,' shrieked the *Mail on Sunday*. In time, 'handbagging' became a byword for the way Thatcher dealt with her political opponents. Her sturdy, smart handbags, almost identical to those used by the Queen, became a potent symbol of her authority, in the same way as Winston Churchill's cigar became his. In fact, Churchill College in Cambridge, created to house his papers, was also chosen by Lady Thatcher to house her letters and speeches, along with some of her famous handbags.

In the office, the style of bag a person carries can be indicative of their position in the hierarchy. A cinematic example of this was powerfully conveyed by Melanie Griffith in *Working Girl* (1988).

As a secretary her squashy shoulder bag is bulging with clutter, but when she starts carrying Sigourney Weaver's streamlined handbags and briefcase Griffith also assumes her boss's business acumen.

S E X   A N D   S T A T U S

For some, caring about one's appearance often leads to conformity, with all the women in a particular social group dressing in similar attire and choosing the same designers. After all, they belong to an elite 'club'. Gilt-strapped society ladies, with their fabulously expensive and logo-embossed bags, are giving much away about their personalities: they wish to make a show of wealth and status.

Handbags can also convey sex and availability, as in the case of overly made-up single girls wearing short skirts and low-cut tops on a night out, who prefer to dance around their handbags rather than carry them. If their purses do represent the female pudenda, then dancing around them in a disco for all to see is tantamount to a mating call.

Observe the handbags of others, and the choices you make yourself. Your handbag announces your arrival and implies a code of conduct. If you have always been a one handbag woman, you might decide that now is an opportunity to use different bags according to the time of day, place and occasion.

CLUTCH The clutch is usually for the evening because it is designed to be slim and held in the hand like a document wallet or tucked neatly under one's arm while holding a glass or being introduced. Discretion is a characteristic of someone choosing this envelope-style bag.

DUFFEL BAG The drawstring top on this bag makes throwing items in and pulling them out easy. Originally a sports bag, the duffel often retains the round or oval base that accommodated a ball.

SHOULDER AND CARTRIDGE BAGS

The long strap allows the shoulders to carry the weight of the bag leaving the hands free to access the contents, making shoulder bags the traditional choice of gamekeepers and postal workers. In fashion terms, the strap is usually slipped over one shoulder so the bag can be shrugged on and off, rather than worn across the body, which distributes the weight more evenly.

HEIRLOOM BAGS Unusual bags – from Bakelite versions to 1950s framed bags – are collectors' items and show an eclectic, individual style. Acquire one of your own by scouring vintage and secondhand shops or simply hunt through your attic for grandma's old handbags.

EVENING BAGS Smaller and more decorative than day bags, these are the bags that give a little more of one's character away. A simple black velvet clutch shows a formal, restrained attitude, while a sparkling, colourful minaudière expresses a more exuberant personality.

KELLY BAG Women do not carry a Kelly bag (whether the real thing from Hermès or one of the many fake imitations) unless they like what it stands for – namely the beauty, wealth, talent and style of Princess Grace.

VANITY CASE The woman who has a specially constructed bag for her stash of creams, lotions and potions is not necessarily vain, but she certainly cares about her appearance.

LOGO-EMBOSSED DESIGNER BAG The owner of this bag aspires to the lifestyle that that particular designer reflects. Do you wish to indulge in a little of the rock-star glamour a Versace bag might bring, or do you prefer a dose of Gallic chic from Chanel?

EMBROIDERED BAGS Loved by those who are arty and prefer quirkiness to uniformity, the delicate embroidered bag is not for those who want a standardized product.

PURSE The bag within a bag, the purse holds money and other precious possessions, such as photographs and documents. A bulging purse shows a busy person who likes to cling on to things, whereas the slim, smart purse reveals a more ordered life and mind.

THE BUCKET BAG (CABOT) A casually chic multitasker, this classic wide-topped bag easily holds a great number of items within its roomy confines. Functional and stylish, the nylon Hervé Chapelier cabot, in particular, is a classic style that merges fashion and practicality, and which is available in an ever-changing range of colours.

MINAUDIÈRE This is the bag as a work of art and is not for the faint-hearted. 'Look at me,' it shouts. The rhinestone-encrusted evening bags by Judith Leiber stand out and demand attention. The word *minaudière* apparently means 'coquettish air', and was coined by Alfred Van Cleef, the jeweller, when he saw Florence Gould, the wife of an American railroad magnate, use a metal cigarette box as a small handbag.

BACKPACK Like the shoulder bag, a backpack allows the weight of the contents to be carried evenly by the body, which is why European children always wear their satchels over both shoulders. In contrast, the traditional British school satchel weighs heavily on one shoulder and is often the reason behind slouches and bad deportment.

During the late 1980s and the 1990s, Miuccia Prada took the backpack from the playground to the front rows of the fashion shows, ensuring that the convenient (and accommodating) rucksack became stylish.

THE TOTE A tote is the perfect grocery or beach bag. The open top reveals an open personality; the contents are easily seen and there is nothing to conceal. Although versions range from the utterly practical to the more stylized, one of the best examples is made by the American company L L Bean. Originally designed to carry ice down from the mountains, the canvas is still treated to make it resistant to mildew.

THE SOCIALITE

Daphne's life is her social diary, but she likes to call it her charity work. Her motto is 'give glamorously', and in doing so she fits in an awful lot of organizational lunches. Every maître d' in town knows her and her small coterie of friends. The contents of her handbag are a testament to her lifestyle, which begins with a little shopping in the morning (on account, of course, and delivered to her home) and a fortifying cup of coffee at her members-only club, where she can read all the gossip columns in peace and quiet. Over lunch she never forgets to take a selenium tablet because simply everyone has told her the supplement keeps old age and sagging skin at bay. In the event of a face-lift, her hair stylist and colourist has promised to tell her which doctor gets the best results — after all, she gets to see all the scars behind the hairline. In the meantime, the 'lady who lunches' gets by with a little designer make-up — she does not like all that trendy matt black packaging, but prefers gilt. Sometimes she will hang on to opera tickets and race meeting cards as mementoes of great parties.

THE CAREER WOMAN

Time is of the essence for the career woman. To fit in with her busy workload, her briefcase has to be streamlined and functional. She has a checklist for the contents of each bag, which she ticks off meticulously: passport, frequent flyer card, mobile phone and currency for tipping. She collects hotel repair kits, so she is never caught with a loose button or hem, and she hangs on to foreign receipts – especially Prada and Gucci – just so she can check how much she saved when she gets home. Hand cream, for a firm but smooth handshake, is her concession to femininity in the boardroom, and strong mints are really for offering to less sweet-smelling business clients. She loves neutral make-up palettes and the classic smell of Chanel No. 5. She could not live without her laptop and Blackberry, but she still likes to have a Montblanc for signing documents.

THE MODEL

Days spent walking from one office to another on 'go-sees' means the young model keeps all her creature comforts to hand in her rucksack. Alongside the essential bottle of mineral water (invariably still and Evian), there is, more often than not, a packet of Marlboro Lights. Sugar-free chewing gum gets rid of smoky breath and a quick spritz of scent will do the rest. Discount cards for cosmetic stores and a collection of lipsticks and eyeshadows given to the model by make-up artists on shoots also make an appearance. A pair of Prada or Tom Ford sunglasses cover up jet-lagged eyes, while reviving aromatherapy sprays combat cabin dehydration. She never carries her mobile phone in her bag, since she's constantly instant-messaging or texting.

THE MOTHER

Since giving birth, the new mother has had a radical life change. Gone is the career bag; she now could not live without her wipe-clean Kate Spade black nylon tote. Keeping calm is of major concern, so she bought a chakra-balancing necklace of semi-precious gems, but cannot wear it because the baby pulls if off. Into the bag goes the necklace, along with a soft toy to pacify the baby, vitamins, reviving essential oils and *The Little Book of Calm*, although she secretly feels that a slick of lipstick and a spray of scent does much more for her spirit than any amount of camomile tea. She has become a member of the nearby museum (it makes walking the baby much more interesting), and her only store card now is for the pharmacy. Seeing all the career girls dashing around town, the mother looks down at her baby in the pushchair and doesn't regret a moment.

THE PARTY GIRL

Life is just one long invitation for the party girl. Late nights and long mornings spent at the hair salon mean a party girl needs every little help she can get to prevent her spirits from flagging. Vitamin sachets keep energy her levels soaring and pick-me-up tonics help to kickstart the day and can even be mixed with champagne for a boosting cocktail.

Maximum-strength tablets eradicate hangover headaches, but on those 'fragile' days she skips the blow-dry (too noisy) and makes do with a ponytail, a pair of shades and a Nars multiple stick to add colour to a sleep-deprived complexion. A Chanel compact and brush is always on standby to banish a shiny nose brought on by dancing too long. The party girl cannot resist her a state-of-the-art smart phone for organizing friends for drinks at one of the bars where she is a member and downloading photos onto her social networking page.

CHAPTER 4

THE **A–Z** OF HANDBAGS

THERE MUST BE AN IMELDA MARCOS OF THE HANDBAG WORLD, A WOMAN WHO HAS BOUGHT ALMOST ALL STYLES AND MAKES OF HANDBAG TO SATISFY HER PASSION FOR HAVING EVERY LABEL, LITERALLY, AT HER FINGERTIPS. HOWEVER, MOST WOMEN SEEM TO BECOME ATTACHED TO A FEW HOUSES AND ADHERE FAITHFULLY TO THEIR DESIGNS. GONE ARE THE DAYS WHEN A WOMAN WOULD HAVE A WARDROBE OF DAY AND EVENING BAGS FROM WHICH TO CHOOSE. FAKE DESIGNER HANDBAGS SPEED UP THE TURNOVER OF POPULAR DESIGNS – AFTER ALL, WHO WANTS TO HANG ON TO A CERTAIN STYLE WHEN EVERYONE HAS ONE? THE RAPID CHANGES IN FASHION MAKE COMPILING A LIST OF COMPANIES AND DESIGNERS A DIFFICULT TASK. FASHION EDITORS, BUYERS AND CURRENT DESIGNERS WERE ASKED FOR THEIR OPINIONS. ALL THE COMPANIES INCLUDED HAVE A STRONG TRADITION THAT MAKES THEM INSTANTLY RECOGNIZABLE BY WOMEN OF DIFFERENT AGES AND NATIONALITIES.

AIGNER
HORSEPLAY

Discreet, though recognizable by the small inverted horseshoe logo, Aigner handbags have always been popular with European women for their simple, elegant shapes and fine workmanship. Etienne Aigner was born in Hungary at the turn of the century but moved to Paris in the 1930s where he learnt the craft of treating and working with leather. By the 1940s he was confident enough to work alone and designed exclusive bags for small Parisian couture houses like Lanvin and Rochas. In the 1950s he moved to New York and began making leather goods under his own name. The company was officially founded in Munich, Germany, in 1965, and Etienne Aigner's monogram was changed slightly into the horseshoe logo that still remains today. By 1975 Etienne Aigner No. 1, the first designer fragrance for men, was launched. The brand's reputation, built on the 'it' bags of the 1950s, '60s and '70s has endured, fusing heritage with contemporary styling.

BILL AMBERG
THE ACCIDENTAL HANDBAG

Although Bill Amberg grew up in Northamptonshire, the home of the English leather trade, he did not plan his career there. In fact, he tried many jobs, including a stint on an oil rig, before moving to Australia in the 1970s where he starting working with a group of leather craftsmen, a liaison which resulted in exhibitions in Sydney, Melbourne and Adelaide. When he returned to the UK in 1982 he set up his own company specializing in leather designs. Amberg has not limited himself to accessories but has diversified into interiors, furniture and corporate products, and with the birth of his second daughter to journalist Susie Forbes, fashion features director of British *Vogue*, he designed a best-selling leather baby holder. Amberg prides himself on blending the elements of traditional craftsmanship with an insight into the modern-day requirements of bags for work, travel and free time.

BALENCIAGA
BIKER-INSPIRED BAGS

Balenciaga bags may look deceptively simple but it's precisely this easy-to-wear quality that have seen them become one of the most sought-after commodities in the fashion world. With handbags crafted from soft vintage lamb or goatskin in the ever-expanding array of signature rainbow shades, any discerning bag lover should have at least one Balenciaga in their collection.

First created by the Spanish designer, Cristóbal Balenciaga, in 1915, the brand has been owned by the Gucci Group since 2001 – the same year that the motorbike-inspired Balenciaga Lariat bag sped onto the fashion scene. Designer Nicholas Ghesquière threw his heart and soul into his first bag under Gucci, distilling his unique vision of biker girl chic into a distressed leather, petrol blue, super-soft tote with tassels, zips and studs. He then rather cunningly dispatched the first batch off to exactly the right friends, namely Kate Moss,

Sienna Miller, Chloë Sevigny and Charlotte Gainsbourg, who unanimously gave the Lariat their seal of approval by flashing it all over town.

Described as the ideal combination of slouchy casualness, but with enough edginess to make it feel bang on-trend, the Lariat is a classic that looks stylish without seeming too try-hard. It has just the right sized leather handles to perch comfortably over your wrist, plus a detachable longer strap for over-the-shoulder toting. Leather laces trail from the front zip and the side to give it a playful edge, but best of all it's the perfect size with an ultra roomy main compartment for all a girls necessities. What more could be asked of a day bag?

LEFT: KOURTNEY KARDASHIAN WITH THE GIANT CITY BAG *RIGHT:* THE ICONIC LARIAT SPAWNED A RANGE OF DESIGNS NOTED FOR THEIR LEATHER LACES, HERE SEEN ON THE FLAP-FRONTED FOLD BAG

BOTTEGA VENETA
THE PIONEER OF WOVEN LEATHER

Renowned for its signature intricately woven leather handbags, Italian accessories powerhouse Bottega Veneta's timeless style has earned it a loyal and discerning following since its launch in 1966. But it was after the company was acquired by the Gucci Group in June 2001, and Tom Ford recruited German designer Tomas Maier to become head of creative design, that the success story really began. Maier has been widely credited with reinventing the label as a benchmark of understated luxury by using the highest quality materials coupled with a simple, label-free aesthetic. Maier's designs have given the label's classic brand of chic a new and decidedly modern perspective. The Cabat bag, a woven leather sack with two handles, was one of the first bags he designed for Bottega Veneta – and has since become one of the label's top-selling items.

Made from four layers of woven napa leather, this open bag is entirely branding and bling-free. To make a Cabat takes two days of hand-weaving leather strands together at

RIGHT: **THE KNOT** CLUTCH
OPPOSITE: **CLASSIC LEATHER WEAVING, LEFT, AND VELVET WITH PAINTED PYTHON IN THE RESINA, RIGHT**

Bottega's factory in Vicenza, Italy. Every inch has to be sized up scientifically – from the leather's colour, texture and strength – to ensure great durability and the softest feel possible. Bottega Veneta's recent designs show enormous restraint with their pared-down feel, but never disappoint. 'I always like an object that is as beautiful on the inside as it is on the outside,' says Maier. 'That's what luxury is all about. It's very personal. Nobody needs to know.'

TORY BURCH
ELEGANCE MADE EASY

Known for its ethos of attainable

luxury as well as the bright orange lacquer doors that feature in every boutique shop, the company was launched in 2004 in Nolita area of New York City by Tory Burch and her then-husband Chris Burch. With an extensive background knowledge in vintage fashion, Tory developed her own brand of beautiful and desirable preppy boho for East Coast ladies.

Vibrant colours make the handbags stand-out style pieces that are versatile enough to with casual or dressy looks. Tory

RIGHT: THE SMALL STRAW BASKET BAG FROM 2011

OPPOSITE: BRETON-INSPIRED NAUTICAL STRIPED BAG

takes a classic shape, such as the postal messenger bag, and gives it urban attitude with chains, or produces a basic style in a variety of finishes, sizes and colours, as with her Robinson collection. Decorated with the T-logo medallion, the bags range from hobos, totes and satchels to clutch, handle and shoulder bags and are in inexpensive materials such as nylon and canvas as well as fine leather and fur; they are generally moderately priced, so there is something for everyone.

BELOW: THE CLASSIC ROBINSON SATCHEL WITH SIGNATURE T-LOGO MEDALLION

Although well known for her handbags, her Reva ballerina shoe won her the Accessories Council of Excellence award in 2007 and acceptance into the CFDA. Her jewellery, denim and ready-to-wear collections are also distinguished by her signature bold patterns and colours, the antithesis of minimalism, and she draws inspiration from art, photography, films, travel and the work of interior designer David Hicks.

BARBOUR
WAXING LYRICAL

Barbour are, of course, more well known for their wax jackets than their handbags, but there was a time in the 1980s when a Barbour cartridge-style bag became a symbol of the London Sloane Ranger. Made from thorn-proof canvas, with leather straps and bindings and brass fastenings, the bags were more often seen in the city than at point-to-points. Key to being a Sloane Ranger was living in close proximity to London's Sloane Square but also having a life in the country at the weekend. A well-used cartridge bag and Barbour jacket for walking up and down the King's Road in the rain was *de rigueur*. The brand has seen a resurgence in the twenty-first century, no doubt due to its associations with Kate Moss and summer music festivals, and the company now makes a variety of tote and satchel bag styles as well as the classic cartridge.

The company was established in South Shields, England, in 1894 by John Barbour, a Scottish farmer, who started using oiled cotton for waterproof clothing, which was made above his small store. Fishermen were among the first to appreciate the cloth, but word soon spread and in 1908 the first Barbour catalogue appeared.

CARTIER
JEWEL IN THE CROWN

In 1901 the Cartier workshops were working at fever pitch to supply 27 diadems that had been ordered from royal courts around the world for the coronation of Edward VII in London. At the time, the future King of England remarked, 'Cartier, jeweller of kings and king of jewellers'. The French company was founded in 1847 but soon became known to a far wider circle than the Parisians because of its unusual designs and fabulous quality. In 1924, for example, Louis Cartier designed the three-band Rolling Ring in honour of his friend Jean Cocteau; the white gold symbolized friendship, the yellow gold loyalty and the pink gold love. However, it was not until 1974 that Cartier decided to launch the Cartier Leather Collection in its distinctive luminous burgundy colour. In 1990, the Panthère theme (a favourite of Wallis Simpson, who first started to wear a Cartier Panthère brooch in 1948) was used in the

LEFT: HAPPY BIRTHDAY. ESTELLE HALLIDAY AND CLAUDIA CARDINALE CARRY THE CARTIER 150TH ANNIVERSARY BAG

leather collection (*see above*). The feline shape was stylized to decorate the clasps, while the linings were spotted in tribute to the panther's coat. In 1997, to celebrate 150 years of Cartier, the Happy Birthday bag (*see opposite, left*) was launched. The burgundy leather, a shade exclusive to Cartier and somewhere between raspberry and wine, was used, with the double C motif embossed in a random pattern like a fireworks display.

CÉLINE
BEST FOOT FORWARD

It is a little-known fact that Céline started in 1946 as a small shop selling children's shoes

and boots in the Rue de Malte, Paris. The Children's Bootery, as it was known, was *the* place to go

for well-heeled families. By 1958 the Céline family started selling the Inca loafer – a French version

of the American penny loafer – adorned with a horse-bit, which quickly

became synonymous with Céline leather goods. Five years later

the family launched the first shoes for women, followed by the

legendary faux-pony print, a design that was picked up again by

Michael Kors (*see also pages 118–9*) in his first collection for

the house in 1998 (*see opposite, top*). Kors' collaboration

with Robert Page, head of design for accessories at

Céline, marked a turning point for the label. Céline

classics have been reinterpreted by using modern

fabrics, including neoprene (*see opposite, far right*). The

MC 1999 shoulder bag from the Plaque Anneau line

is a prime example; 5,000 have been bought every

year for the past 30 years.

The same can be said of the two other Céline essentials

that have stood the test of time, namely the simple

tote with its circular handles and the Omega

1427 with extendible sides that can be worn

over the shoulder or hand-held.

Although Michael Kors left in 2003, after turning around the

accessory line, the brand has gone from strength to strength under

the guidance of Phoebe Philo, appointed creative director in 2008.

Simple and refined, her iconic styles for the brand

emphasize quality and function, and

include the classic Box Bag from

2009 and the flamboyant

Trapeze from 2011.

CHANEL
THE CHAIN GANG

Of all the 'must-haves' that every modern woman aspires to, a gilt-chained Chanel bag is certainly one. The distinctive chain shoulder strap, threaded with leather, was inspired by Coco Chanel's use of flat-sided chains that were sewn into the hems of her jackets to help them hang beautifully. Although Coco Chanel started designing in July 1915, when she opened her *maison de couture* in Biarritz, France, she did not design handbags until 1955. In fact, she had closed her atelier in Rue Cambon, Paris, in 1939 with the onset of the Second World War and only re-opened it in 1953 when prompted by the company that sold her perfumes, by which time she was 70 years old.

The first handbags were made in jersey and leather in shades of beige, brown, navy and black. The quilting technique is thought to have been a way of making the jersey – her signature material – more suitable for the purpose of a handbag, but was also used for leather versions. The linked C logo was not on the original bags (*see below, left*) and was only added in the late 1960s, but the original 2.55 quilted bag was relaunched to great fanfare in 2005. Since Karl Lagerfeld has been at the helm of Chanel, many inventive and humorous bags have been designed, such as ones with clips to hold newspapers and the

ABOVE: **C OR NOT 2 C – NAOMI CAMPBELL ON THE CATWALK**

brightly coloured sheepskin bags of winter 1997 (*see right*). The 1998 Chanel bag, the revolutionary 2005 (*see opposite*), had a rigid frame but was shaped to fit the contours of the body and could even be used as a pillow.

82

HERVÉ CHAPELIER
FRENCH REVOLUTION

Chapelier means 'hatter' in French, but that did not stop Hervé Chapelier from deciding to concentrate on another kind of accessory – handbags. Born in 1950 in the fashionable French resort of Biarritz, Hervé grew up surrounded by the stylish people who holidayed there. Although his education in Bordeaux did not involve design and, in fact, he went to business school, an artistic streak runs through the family; one sister is an artist and the other is a florist. At the age of 26, Hervé created a light, useful duffel bag from pieces of nylon, which was an instant hit – not just for being lightweight but also for coming in a huge range of colours. He followed it up with his famous lightweight two-tone trapeze-shaped bag. His mini-rucksack enjoyed the same fame. His bags work so well and are loved by many women because they look equally stylish at the gym or the office, with jeans or a suit. The contrasting colourways and sturdy saddle stitching sets them apart from his many imitators. Hervé Chapelier was the first handbag designer to make nylon cool and desirable – something Prada did only 15 years later.

CHLOÉ
BOHO-CHIC FOR COOL GIRLS

Founded in Paris in 1952 by Egyptian-born designer Gaby Aghion as an alternative to haute couture, Chloé have always represented a more adventurous, bohemian style, and has list of past designers that reads like a who's who of fashion, including the likes of Karl Lagerfeld and Stella McCartney. But it was when head designer Phoebe Philo joined in 2001 that the label decided to launch their first range of handbags. Success followed quickly – their seductive combination of novelty, femininity and functionality made Chloé's elegant handbags instant must-haves. Indeed, arguably one of the most sought after 'it' bags of all time, the Paddington, with its distinctive oversized lock and doctor's briefcase shape, was released by the brand in 2005. It sold out before a single one made it to the boutique's shelves – and even now is still a popular pick, having assumed

BELOW: **A** VARIETY OF STYLES, FROM CHAIN-STRAP TO POUCHETTE TO BUCKET classic status among handbag aficionados. Indeed the Paddington is still mostly available only by means of a very long waiting list.

The clever idea behind the bag was to counter the fact that designer clothes had become so accessible and widely copied by creating a strictly limited-edition piece that, as well as costing well over the average monthly salary, would make a woman feel part of an exclusive club. Other notable bag designs include the Bracelet, Betty and Edith – and with designer Clare Waight Keller at the reins, who claims to design for 'real girls', the theme of laid-back but ladylike bags continues apace.

COACH
THE AMERICAN DREAM

In true stars-and-stripes style, the American company Coach started with a baseball glove. When the founder of Coach first discovered the distinctive markings and qualities of the leather that was being used to make baseball gloves – and its incredible suppleness despite hard wear and rough handling – he decided that it would be perfect for handbags. The leather was refined slightly, but left natural to allow the grain to show and burnish beautifully with age. The year was 1941 and at the time the idea was quite revolutionary among the smart American women of the day.

The business was originally a family-run affair of six artisans, who operated from a Manhattan loft. The company is still based in midtown Manhattan and the leather artisans are considered among the best in the USA. The company's philosophy has remained steadfastly the same: their bags must have the unique, clean Coach look that is immediately identifiable. They must be handmade using organic leather that is completely 'naked', so it burnishes easily and takes on the rich patina of a well-worn saddle.

Coach, who celebrated their 70th anniversary in 2011, is to handbags

what Levi's is to jeans – an American classic.

CONNOLLY
A DRIVING FORCE

If you have ever been driven in a Rolls Royce, Aston Martin, Ferrari or Morgan, then you have already come into contact with Connolly. This exclusive British company began upholstering coaches and cars in 1878 when two brothers, Samuel and Joseph Connolly, opened for business. Soon after, they were commissioned by the Palace to make leather seats for Edward VII's Coronation Coach. After 117 years of supplying the finest leather to prestige marques as well as to private customers, Connolly decided to broaden their horizons and enter the world of luxury leather goods. In 1995 the Connolly shop – designed by Andrée Putman – was opened in the old Belgravia Stables in London. The sleek Connolly City rucksack (see *opposite, far right*) was worn and recognized by women in the know – usually those who grew up being

driven to school every
day in the Roller. Although
the leather goods business
closed in 2002, the brand still
exists as a bespoke retailer.

90

DIOR
A CHRISTIAN FOLLOWING

Christian Dior was 41 in 1946 when he opened the couture house at 30, Avenue Montaigne, Paris, under his own name. His first collection the following year was dubbed the New Look by Carmel Snow, the influential editor of *Harper's Bazaar,* and since then the house of Dior quickly moved into other areas of design and accessories, including perfumery, jewellery, tableware, cosmetics and babywear.

In 1957, Yves St Laurent replaced Christian Dior, who had been struck down by a sudden heart attack. Subsequent designers for Dior have been Marc Bohan, Gianfranco Ferrè and, until 2011, John Galliano. Galliano injected freshness while continuing to keep the unashamedly feminine feel and look that is so very Dior and which can be seen clearly in the handbags.

In 1996, Dior sponsored the Cezanne exhibition at the National Galleries of the Grand Palais, which was inaugurated by a gala dinner attended by the late Diana, Princess of Wales. That evening she carried the best-selling classic Dior bag (*see above*). The four fobs spelling D. I. O. R. hang from the handle and make the handbag instantly recognizable. After that night the bag was renamed the Lady Dior as a tribute to Diana. Another iconic bag, the Miss Dior, was launched in 2011.

CARLOS FALCHI
PATCHWORK EXOTICS

Known for super-soft, vibrant, slouchy leather bags in patchwork combinations of exotic skins, including python, alligator and ostrich, as well as in fringing and fur, the Brazilian-born Carlos Falchi began his career in Greenwich Village, New York City, in the 1970s while working as a busboy at Max's Kansas City. He was soon creating handbags that featured low-key casual shapes, which encapsulated the effortless attitude of the decade, and designed for Henri Bendel, Neiman Marcus and Bergdorf Goodman. Free of logos and noticeable hardware, his handmade bags are for the busy woman, as they have large interior pockets and compartments. In fact, he has said, 'I want to be able to squash and trash a bag and still see it keep going.'

In 1980 *Women's Wear Daily* declared his Buffalo satchel the most-copied bag in the industry. Unconstructed and unlined, it was made from a single skin with only two seams. Falchi has been at the leading edge of producing environmentally controlled farm-bred exotic skins and works with tanneries to develop new techniques that are protective of the world's ecosystems.

He has also produced lower-priced lines, including one for the American retailer Target in 2009, and Chi by Falchi. He designs accessories for the catwalk for Donna Karan, Vera Wang, Ralph Rucci and Bill Blass and for the television series *Lipstick Jungle* and the 2008 *Sex and the City* movie. Several of his designs are part of the permanent collection of the Costume Institute of the Metropolitan Museum of Art.

OPPOSITE: **A 2008 PATCHWORK REPTILE BAG** *RIGHT: :* **THE ICONIC BUFFALO BAG IN OSTRICH**

F E N D I
T H E   R O M A N   E M P I R E

Fendi's fame and fortune goes back to small beginnings. In 1925, two brothers, Edoardo and Adele Fendi, began making fur coats and small leather goods from their workshop in Via del Plebiscito in Rome, but it was not until 1946 that they opened a shop. Their five sisters, Anna, Paola, Franca, Carla and Alda, then joined the business and became the driving force behind the company's success. Their first stroke of genius was to take Karl Lagerfeld on board to design the furs in 1965. He played down the heavy, old-style, status-symbol look of traditional fur coats and used inlaying, varnishing and interweaving to give the coats a fresh, young, fashionable feel. The leather goods underwent a similar transformation, and when the president of Bloomingdale's saw the accessories while in Rome, he decided to take Fendi to the USA.

The double F logo became an instant hit and Fendi took off internationally. In the 1970s the company developed a special etched leather they called *granapaglia,* which was very supple, durable and instantly recognizable. Historically, their best-selling items were the Catherine Deneuve bag, which was specially created for the actress, and the Baguette (*see opposite*), which became adored by the fashion pack. Called the Baguette because the shorter shoulder strap meant it sat under the arm like a loaf of French bread, the bag was made in a variety of materials from woven raffia to cow-print pony hair – one version for every day of the week. Hot on the heels – or rather from the oven – of the Baguette came the Croissant (*see above right*). The roomy Spy, with braided handles and ultra-rich, soft leather, was a celebrity favourite when launched in 2005 as was the B bag with it's oversized Perspex buckles from 2006, which was worn by Kate Hudson, Reese Witherspoon and Paris Hilton.

SALVATORE FERRAGAMO
SHOEMAKER TO THE STARS

It is impossible to talk about Salvatore Ferragamo without talking about shoes. Although there are now fashion shows, fragrances and shops, Ferragamo will always be inextricably linked to footwear, and handbags and small leather goods were a natural progression. Salvatore Ferragamo was born to a poor family in 1898 in the small village of Bonito, near Naples, Italy. He wanted to become a shoemaker and made his first pair for his sister's Holy Communion when he was just nine years old. In 1914 he joined his three brothers in Santa Barbara, California, where they opened a shoe-repair shop. The burgeoning movie studios in the area became the source of much of their work and Salvatore soon had Mary Pickford and Rudolph Valentino among his clients. He returned to Italy in 1936, settling in Florence and exporting to the USA.

During the Second World War and the Fascist period, heavy restrictions were placed on raw materials. As a result, Ferragamo quickly started to experiment with unusual mediums, such as cork, which he used to create the first wedge shoes, and nylon fishing line, with which he fashioned his famous 'invisible' shoe. This innovative style extends to the handbags, which in recent years have made use of such unexpected materials as Perspex and aluminium. He died prematurely in 1960, leaving his wife Wanda and their children to continue and expand the business. Ferragamo shoes and handbags are synonymous with 'made in Italy' style and quality.

G U C C I

H ITTING THE G S POT

The first thing you notice is the snaffle. It is there on the belts, the loafers and the handbags.

Gucci originally traded as saddlers and is proud of its horsey, well-heeled roots. That is not to say

the company has always enjoyed the cult status of today. In 1990 Dawn Mello was brought in from

the New York store Bergdorf Goodman to revamp a label that had fallen into the luxury trap.

Everybody who wanted a Gucci handbag had one because fakes were rife. After eliminating 10,000

of the more dubiously designed products, Mello appointed Tom Ford, the American designer known

for his pared-down, stylishly sexy clothes. Ford's first show in 1995 went down as a 'fashion moment'

– the models, the clothes and, most importantly, the handbags were to die for.

A Gucci bag was once again as covetable as it had been in the 1950s when

Audrey Hepburn, Grace Kelly and

Brigitte Bardot carried them.

100

LEFT: KATE MOSS ON THE CATWALK

Although Tom Ford, who departed in 2004, used the traditional bamboo handles and snaffle decoration, he cleverly updated them for the new customer without alienating the old (*see this page and opposite*). Bamboo was paired with slinky python or afghan fur, while the snaffle was stylized into more abstract forms that transport it from the tack box to something more sculptural and sexy. Gucci also continues its tradition of releasing 'named' styles, such as the Sienna hobo bag, named after Sienna Miller.

LULU GUINNESS
LIFE'S A BAG OF ROSES

When Lulu Guinness left her job in a video production company in 1989, she could not possibly have hoped for the success she has enjoyed in the years that followed. From the basement of her house in West London she began creating whimsical handbags that have become works of art.

Two of her signature floral handbags, the Florist Basket (see *right*) and the Violet Hanging Basket, became part of the permanent fashion collection at the Victoria & Albert Museum in London. Her Lips clutch is a fashion favourite and available in a huge range of materials and colours, including snakeskin and Perspex, and finished in metallics, studs and crystals.

In 1995 she opened a shop with the fashion designer Selina Blow in Pimlico, London, and a year later opened her own salon in Ledbury Road, Notting Hill. She now has shops in London, New York and Tokyo, and designs the interiors herself. Her client list includes Helena Bonham Carter, Dita von Teese, Katy Perry, Sophie Dahl, Keira Knightly and Alexa Chung.

Lulu Guinness loves old-style glamour and this is reflected in her handbags, which make heavy use of unusual trims, beading and embroidery. She employs a team of ladies living in the English countryside who hand-embroider her bags. The emphasis she places on old-fashioned excellence is carried through to the service in her shops. Every customer who has ever bought a bag receives a card that entitles them to use the ladies' room, drop off heavy bags, shelter from the rain or have a cup of tea in the shop. Lulu Guinness offers her customers the same kind of care and attention to detail that have made her delicately feminine bags so successful the whole world over.

NATHALIE HAMBRO

ARTS AND CRAFTS

You would be forgiven for not knowing who Nathalie Hambro is, or where her bags are sold; few of her pieces get passed the auction houses and museums that exhibit them. In London, both

Sotheby's and the Victoria & Albert Museum have shown her work. Designed, made and finished by her own hand, Hambro creates unusual, sculptural bags that defy fashion and make light of practicality. Some of her designs, such as the bronze mesh Cabat bag, are too fragile to use, while her Japanese Inro bags are simply too beautiful to put to practical use.

All of her pieces are memorable works of art, and for this reason she designs handbags and jewellery for the couture house of Balmain. Although Hambro is French-born, she has lived in England for the past 26 years and has adopted British nationality. One of her first designs was an aluminium lunchbox, based on traditional Indian tiffin boxes. It became a cult item and is just one of many examples of how Nathalie takes the ordinary and transforms it into something extraordinary.

HERMÈS
RIDING HIGH

The approach they adopt at Hermès is that shaking up tradition is the only way to respect it. The company began in 1837 when Thierry Hermès opened a workshop for horse and harness equipment after training at Pont Audemer, the main centre for leather work in France. His second son, Charles Emile, assisted him, and won a prize for design at the Paris World Fair in 1878, which helped him to open a saddlery at the prestigious address 24, Rue Fauberg Saint-Honoré. Hermès soon began to supply the courts of Europe, and the tradition for excellence and working for royalty began. However, it was Grace Kelly in the 1950s who gave Hermès the worldwide recognition it has now. During her engagement to Prince Rainier of Monaco, she was photographed many times with her favourite Hermès bag, which the company renamed 'the Kelly' when they wed. That particular style of bag was originally designed in 1892 as a 'roomy, trapezoidal leather bag with a clasp, intended to hold a rider's saddle and boots', but in 1930 Emile Hermès made a smaller 46-cm (18-inch) version for women, which became the 'ladies' travel bag with strap'. Other bags, such as the Bugatti and the Birkin, have become equally covetable.

In 1997 the Belgian-born designer Martin Margiela was appointed designer for the ready-to-wear business, but the accessory side continues to make news. In the late 1990s Hermès collaborated with the Yawanawas tribe of Brazilian Indians to work with a new substance called Amazonia, a plant-based material made from hevea sap that could be applied to cotton cloth. Amazonia shares many of the same qualities as leather – it is a natural, living material and does not tear. Hermès has used the material to great acclaim in the Herbag design (*see opposite*). The company continues to thrive in the twenty-first century, with the Birkin and Kelly making unprecedented comebacks.

RIGHT: MODEL ELLE MACPHERSON

A N Y A **H I N D M A R C H**

BUY IT WITH A BOW

Anya Hindmarch's first love began at 14 – it was with an old Gucci handbag given to her by her mother. At 17 she went to Florence to learn Italian and returned with a leather drawstring bag that she had noticed all the Florentine women carrying. A year later, Anya Hindmarch was designing and selling her first collection of handbags. The first stroke of luck – or first sign of success to come – was when she designed a bag for a reader's offer in British *Harpers & Queen*, which generated 500 orders. Hindmarch is quintessentially English and there is always something quirky about her designs – she has injected humour into the handbag and that is what makes her different. She has become known for her creative projects, too, including the eco-friendly I'm Not A Plastic Bag in 2007.

MARC JACOBS
QUIRKY, COOL, INDIE

A born and bred New Yorker, Marc Jacobs attended Parsons School of Design, where he won plaudits that included Design Student of the Year. Jacobs created his first collection in 1986 with his long-term business partner Robert Duffy, before joining Perry Ellis, where his groundbreaking 1992 Grunge collection won him critical acclaim but saw him dismissed from the brand.

In 1997 he became creative director of Louis Vuitton, where he has spearheaded blockbuster handbag collaborations with Stephen Sprouse and Takashi Murakami, though

RIGHT: **BOWLING BAG STYLE**
OPPOSITE: **THE STAM**

his eponymous brand is noted for it's covetable 'it' bags, such as the Venetia, with its doctor shape and buckled pockets, and the Stam, probably the most enduring style to date. Named after Canadian model Jessica Stam, the bag is available in sequinned, stardust, quilted and metallic finishes as well as in 'mini' sizes, and is handmade by 9–10 Italian craftspeople.

Known for fun and youthfulness – *New York Times* has said of his first collection that it was 'kids' clothes for grown-ups' – his handbags follow the same ethos. His choice of models and the presentation of his ad campaigns, photographed by Juergen Teller, underline his quirky offbeat humour and indie style, and have included Victoria Beckham, Sophia Coppola, Dakota Fanning, Helena Bonham Carter and Wynona Ryder. In his words, his designs are 'a little preppie, a little grungy, a little couture'. In 2010 *Time* magazine named him as one of the 100 most influential people in the world.

D O N N A **K A R A N**
T A K I N G I T E A S Y

It is easy to see why fashion designer Donna Karan is called 'the Queen of New York'. Women look up to her, and her designs, because she knows what women want – simple pieces, like stretch-jersey bodies and wrap-around skirts that make them look slimmer and can be worn with the minimum of fuss.

Fashion design and clothes are a part of Donna's lifeblood. Her stepfather was in the Seventh Avenue rag trade, her father was a tailor and her mother, Helen 'Richie' Faske, was a model. Donna worked for Anne Klein, then set up her own business in 1985 with her sculptor husband Stephan Weiss. Her aim was to create a 'compromise between tailoring and sportswear', and her diffusion range DKNY serves the sportswear aspect while the Donna Karan label provides the tailoring approach. Her handbags also meet this brief. Whatever the fabric or design, a Donna Karan handbag will always serve its purpose while looking smart and stylish.

ORLA KIELY

IRISH CHARM

Orla Kiely makes great use of vibrant colours, patterns and unusual materials and shapes to create handbags that are both practical and fresh in design.

Raised in Dublin, Ireland, Orla Kiely first showed artistic promise at the local convent school that she attended. After studying at the Royal College of Art, where she gained a masters degree in textiles, Orla then went on to work for such blue-chip companies as Habitat, Marks & Spencer and Esprit before starting up her own label. Her laminated-cloth totes with their easily recognizable patterns catapulted her into the spotlight. She has also expanded into clothing, fragrance, homewares, furniture, wallpaper and stationery.

CALVIN KLEIN

MASTER OF THE MINIMAL

Calvin Klein knows how to create a scandal. In the 1970s he did it with an advertisement for his jeans showing Brooke Shields and the words, 'Nothing comes between me and my Calvins'. In the 1990s he did it once again with the startling black-and-white photographs for his unisex scent cKone, showing Kate Moss and anti-fashion, anti-hero types huddled in groups, united only by the whiff of the cologne.

The words invariably used to describe his clothes are 'minimal', 'pared-down' and 'beautifully cut'. Calvin Klein's emphasis on simple cut and comfortable materials have made both his clothing and underwear lines immensely wearable and popular. His black label Collection line is high-end designer, while his cK Calvin Klein grey label is a diffusion range with shoes and handbags that closely follow the vagaries of fashion, but are tempered to fit the casual simplicity of the line by the use of hardwearing materials in just a few colours.

MICHAEL KORS
CLEAN-CUT AMERICAN CHIC

With a career that began with women's ready-to-wear in the 1980s, Michael Kors rapidly gained prominence as the creative director for Céline during the late 1990s, where he was noted for bringing the accessories line of the brand into critical acclaim (see pages 76–7). In 2001 he launched his first fully fledged accessories line and in 2004 he debuted the sportswear line Michael Michael Kors, the same year he showed his final collection for Céline. His clothes were recognized by Anna Wintour, editor of American *Vogue*, as being created in the American sportswear tradition of Norman Norell and Bill Blass. Kors' luxe uptown tailoring carries over to his handbag line too, with styles such as the timelessly elegant Quinn satchel and clutch or the Gia shoulder bag. With shapes that are roomy and practical and colours that are usually muted and neutral, these are classically elegant handbags that can be worn every day with a variety of daywear, from casual denim to ladylike shifts and suits. Often noted as a designer for the 'jet-set' classes, he appropriately enough produces a range of flight bags.

Kors takes inspiration from such thoroughbred American beauties as Jacqueline Kennedy Onassis, Gwyneth Paltrow and Ali MacGraw, with his clothes worn by a huge selection of red-carpet celebrities such as Jennifer Aniston, Jennifer Lopez and Catherine Zeta-Jones, as well as First Lady Michelle Obama.

LAUNER
HOLDING THE ROYAL
PURSE STRINGS

Whether the Queen is on official business in India, spending a day at Ascot or attending the State Opening of Parliament, the sturdy, practical handbags fitting neatly over her arm are always Launer. Needless to say, the company prefers longevity and luxury rather than fleeting fashions and eye-catching trends. Form, function and quality are the tenets of Gerald Bodmer's company, founded just over 50 years ago. Surprisingly, Bodmer started his career as a musician, studying the clarinet at the Royal College of Music in London and

LEFT: A SOLDIER LOOKS AFTER HER MAJESTY'S HANDBAG AT THE TROOPING OF THE COLOUR working with the Carla Rosa Opera Company and the BBC. When he left, he went into commerce and learnt the leather-goods trade at a company which, at the time, held the royal warrant for the Queen Mother. Some time later, he founded his own company, manufacturing handmade handbags and personal leather goods for such prestigious British brands as Mappin & Webb, Asprey and Russell & Bromley. The company later received the royal warrant to Her Majesty Queen Elizabeth II for handbags.

After the Queen appeared at the Royal Wedding of Prince William and Kate Middleton in April 2011 carrying a bespoke cream leather Launer bag, sales rose 60 per cent.

J U D I T H   L E I B E R
F R O M   B A G S   T O   R I C H E S

Judith Leiber's life has all the makings of a Spielberg movie. Born in 1921 to an upper middle-class Jewish family of jewellers in Budapest, Hungary, she won a place at King's College, Cambridge, to read chemistry. Her studies were cut short by the Second World War, which prevented her returning to England after visiting her family in Hungary. By various twists of fate, her family escaped the concentration camps during the Nazi occupation. Her mother and sister would dirty their faces and don babushkas, pretending to be old women in order to avoid the unwanted attention of German soldiers. Judith joined the Hungarian Handbag Guild as the first-ever female apprentice and was kept busy cooking glue and sweeping floors.

One day in 1945, Judith bumped into a friend who was with an American GI, Gerson Leiber. A year later she married him and moved to New York. Judith worked for several handbag manufacturers before eventually plucking up enough courage to start her own business in 1963. Although she makes day bags – albeit very expensive alligator ones – she is more famous for

her evening bags, which are covered in anything up to 10,000 Austrian

crystal rhinestones. The bags have been a favourite with America's First

Ladies, including Jackie Kennedy, Hillary Clinton, Barbara Bush

and Nancy Reagan (who gave one to

Raisa Gorbachev) because they remain a symbol

of American quality and workmanship.

The extraordinary amount of work that

goes into making one of Leiber's minaudières

is legendary. Some of them use over 10,000

rhinestones, which are painstakingly applied one by one, and

can take more than a week to complete. Each bag contains a

miniature comb, purse and mirror. The wealth of designs – from doves of peace to mark the end of the Gulf War (*see below*) to rosebuds and polar bears – means the bags fast become collectors' items. In 1997 the Victoria & Albert Museum in London added one of Judith Leiber's Fabergé Egg bags to its collection. Not surprisingly, when Bernice Norman, from New Orleans, loaned her collection of 300 Leiber minaudières to the city's Museum of Art, a remarkable 10,000 people queued up to see them. Unlike most handbags, a Leiber creation can be guaranteed not only to serve a purpose to its owner, but to entertain those who surround her.

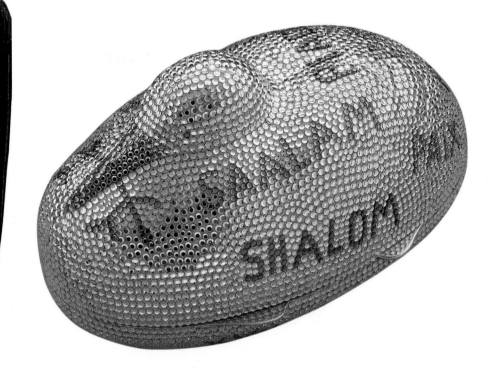

LOEWE
SOFT, SENSUAL AND SPANISH

The blueprint for Loewe style is supple, butter-soft leather made sexy. Although Loewe is sometimes called the Hermès of Spain, Enrique Loewe did not start out as a saddler. From the first day he started trading in 1846, out of his small shop in Calle del Tobo in the Spanish capital of Madrid, he sold small, exquisitely made handbags and accessories. By 1905 the King and Queen of Spain had become patrons, and their descendants, King Juan Carlos and his family, are still customers today. In 1947 Loewe became the sole distributor of Christian Dior's New Look clothing in Spain and only then became interested in designing a fashion line. When the company did so, in the 1960s, they specialized in creating flawlessly soft leather trousers, jackets and skirts in unusual but beautiful colours. The label was given a refreshing injection of style by the appointment of Stuart Vevers in 2007, who relaunched the hallmark Amazona bag in 2010.

LONGCHAMPS
QUINTESSENTIALLY FRENCH

Walk along any street in France and you cannot help but spot fashionable women carrying Longchamp bags, known for being unpretentious and wonderfully useful, yet at the same time being rather smart and stylish. One of the most popular, the Pliage bag, is a folding nylon shopper that is trimmed in cowhide and has sold over a million since it was launched in 1994.

Founded in 1948 by Jean Cassegrain, the company originally specialized in leather-covered pipes. Over time the range was expanded to include humidors, ashtrays and pipe-holders. By 1970 Longchamps was producing a hugely successful nylon and leather luggage line. In 1998 the company celebrated 50 years in business with the 50th Anniversary bag, made in genuine crocodile with a lambskin lining and gold plate bamboo lock and in 2011 Kate Moss designed a collection for the brand.

ALEXANDER MCQUEEN
DARK GLAMOUR

With his death in February 2010, Alexander 'Lee' McQueen left the fashion world bereft of a visionary. A background in fine tailoring combined with an unconventional mind led to couture and ready-to-wear designs that were theatrical, darkly glamorous, emotionally powerful and complicated in their construction.

Like his clothing collections, McQueen's handbags are recognized by their dramatic and multilayered embellishment. Understated they are not. His clutches in particular emphasize the gothic elements so readily associated with his work: skulls, jewels, fantastic layerings of embellishment and bling. A few, such as the Cathedral Skull and Knuckle box clutches, look like ancient treasures or talismans from some supernatural world or the afterlife – indeed, some of the names chosen for his bags evoke exactly such a world, as in the case of the Wicca. The Union Jack, an image as much associated with McQueen as the skull, has also made an appearance in various guises on the clutch.

The handbags are often squat, squashy shapes, such as the iconic Novak bag, which has been updated since its first incarnation, or possess a tough rock-chic attitude, such as the Biker shoulder bag or chain-handled Faithful bucket tote. The remarkable De Manta was inspired by the stingray but also looks vaguely bat-like. Today the brand continues its success at Gucci under the leadership of Sarah Burton.

OPPOSITE: **PYTHON SKULL KNUCKLE CLUTCH WITH SWAROVSKI CRYSTALS**
RIGHT: **THE SQUASHY GOLD ELIVE BAG**

MULBERRY

THE HUNTIN', SHOOTIN' AND FISHIN' BAG

Mulberry is all things English. The country squire style has been carefully cultivated by Mulberry's founder and designer, Roger Saul. Although Mulberry has the air of a company that has been around for generations, it was actually

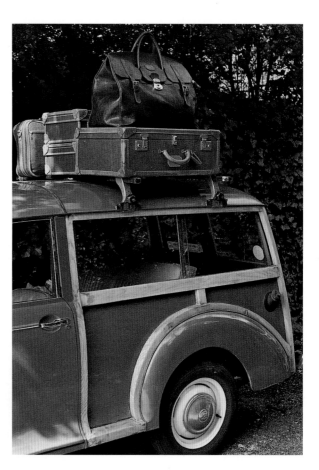

established in 1969 when Roger started making chokers and belts based on horse tackle on the kitchen table of his flat. His girlfriend Monty, who later became his wife, was a model, and she successfully launched his designs by wearing them with very little else. By 1971 Roger had a staff of 16 craftsmen working in an old forge near Bath, using traditional leather-making skills.

The sportsmen theme carried through to both the fashion and home collections. The popular, stylish Grand Despatch bag and Binocular bag, which brought a little of the countryside to the city, have both become modern classics, while notable 'it' bags in the twenty-first century included the Roxanne, Alexa and Bayswater. The company has also collaborated with a slew of leading-edge designers, including Luella Bartley, Giles Deacon and Julie Verhoeven.

OSPREY
A VILLAGE AFFAIR

After working in the fashion industry, it was colour – or rather, lack of it – that made Graeme Ellisdon decide to set up his own company making belts and gloves in a full spectrum of lively hues and shades. He and his younger sister, Bain, taught themselves to plait, cut and stitch leather in a tiny room above a small barn in their home village of Kimpton in Hertfordshire, England. As orders grew, Graeme began to pass on his techniques to local villagers. The local craftspeople would drop by in the morning to pick up their work for the day then deliver it, once completed, in the afternoon. This kind of cottage industry was perfect for the high-quality, hand-finished product Osprey has come to represent. By 1990, Graeme had designed his first handbag, the small suede Tiffany, which was followed by the Dolly. He prefers not to use metal clasps, fastenings or trinkets so that the form of the bag is what catches the eye rather than the details. In his view, 'a woman likes to be perceived by the outward appearance of her handbag, but it is the contents that reveal what she's really like'. The diffusion line, O.S.P Osprey, was launched in 2006.

PRADA
THE ITALIAN JOB

The black nylon zip bag

with gilt chain handles captured the hearts of the fashionable post-1980s crowd, who were tired of the flashier designer bags and hungry for something new. Nylon was the antidote: it was anti-fashion – both industrial and modern – but was made desirable and reassuringly expensive in the form of the Prada bag.

Since 1913, the Fratelli Prada had been making luggage and handbags for the well-to-do

Milanese. Their shop near the Duomo was fitted with mahogany and brass fittings made in England. The family business was founded on excellent products, but nothing in the range was particularly exciting. When Miuccia Prada joined the company in 1978 as a designer and shareholder, she decided to turn tradition on its head and make the company more a reflection of her own uncompromising and eclectic style, which can be described as rich bohemian. She loves combining

LEFT: A DISCREET, LADYLIKE, STRUCTURED STYLE FEATURES UNEXPECTED COLOUR

luxury with the unconventional and adding a little humour. This is seen in her Miu Miu range. Each season, when the fashion pack descend on Milan for the fashion collections, editors and stylists rush to the shop to stock up on the latest shoes, boots and handbags. Along with Gucci, Prada has redefined Italian style, making it less *signorile* and more cutting edge than it has ever been. To the fashion cognoscenti, the *Borsa di Milano* (translated literally as the 'Milan bag') no longer means the Italian stock-exchange: it simply means Prada.

Trend-setting colours and shapes that have timeless glamour define the Prada bag. A classic example of this is the Gauffre line of ruched leather bags – a celebrity favourite but also a classic.

RIGHT: **THE ICONIC NYLON RUCKSACKS WITH THEIR DISCREET TRIANGLE LOGO, FIRST LAUNCHED IN 1985**

YVES SAINT LAURENT
CUTTING ABOVE

Yves Saint Laurent was born on 1 August, 1936, in Oran, Algeria, but left for Paris after his baccalaureate. He wanted to be a fashion designer and showed his drawings to Michel de Brunhoff, a director of *Vogue*, who used some of them in the magazine and who also introduced this young talented man to Christian Dior. Yves worked for Dior until his death in 1957, when he took over as art director at Christian Dior, and his first collection was a phenomenal success. In 1958 he met Pierre Berge, who became his business partner in 1961 when they formed the house of Yves Saint Laurent. His 'smoking' jacket for women has become a classic,

and he was the first designer to be

honoured by an exhibition at the Metropolitan

Museum of Art in New York in 1983, organized

by ex-*Vogue* editor, Diana Vreeland.

Modernity through timelessness is the

key to his much-copied designs.

KATE SPADE
INSIDER INFORMATION

The criterion for a Kate Spade bag is, 'if it will be out of style tomorrow, it won't be added to the line today'. Kate's sage words are the fruit of five years' experience working as fashion accessories editor of *Mademoiselle* magazine, from 1986 to 1991. The experience made her realize that there were not enough no-nonsense bags with a sense of wit and propriety, so she set about solving the problem with her husband Andy Spade. Naturally, both the press and public fell for her light, nylon bags in easy shapes and have been enchanted by her more unusual designs, which draw inspiration from sources as diverse as beach umbrellas, Harris tweed coats and childhood memories. The real thing is distinguished by the black-and-white label. The logo is true to Kate's simple style and practical designs, which is exactly why modern women love the bags.

PAURIC SWEENEY
ARCHITECTURAL BALANCE

One of the hottest handbag designers of the first decade of the twenty-first century, Irish-born Pauric Sweeney actually read architecture at university, but left his studies early in favour of setting up a design studio in East London – to the delight of handbag-lovers everywhere!

Launched in 2004, Pauric Sweeney bags were instantly snapped up by leading department stores and boutiques internationally. Then in the summer of 2005 the designer moved his atelier to Florence, Italy, to work closely with prestigious Italian tanneries and master leather craftsmen.

His architectural roots can be seen everywhere in the sleek, balanced structure of the fabulous bags. This compelling combination of form and function has meant that his handbags are craved by some of the most discerning shoppers around, including Madonna and Kate Winslet. Very minimal in cut, but bold in texture, each Pauric Sweeney handbag has heaps of personality from base to handle – making it the perfect statement piece. The bags are loved by women of all ages looking for a classic yet directional product that does not have

flashy logos or ubiquitously available fakes. Key shapes are his classic doctor's bags and structured totes with metallic finishes, but they're also notoriously hard to get hold of in the high street, and boutique internet sites are often the only way to find these sought-after handbags.

Meanwhile, luxury fashion companies including Givenchy, Loewe and Christian Lacroix have courted Sweeney, but for now the defiantly independent leather genius is happy remaining at his own brand – and long may he stay.

OPPOSITE: **THE MADAME BRIEFCASE IN ZEBRA-PRINTED PONYSKIN** *RIGHT:* **THE MADAME CLUTCH IN LIZARD**

TANNER KROLLE

ART OF LEATHERCRAFT

This discreet British company has been making classic leather goods for over 150 years and has a rich history in saddlery and luggage (Diana, Princess of Wales, travelled with Tanner Krolle). One of the world's finest leather goods firms, they are specialists in bespoke and custom-made products and keep the company's strong heritage but with a modern slant. The Tanner Krolle woman is 'aged between 25 and 45, she's urban, independent, successful, confident, stylish, sensual, intelligent and elegant… appreciates quality … and wants a bag that isn't a badge… rejects anything flashy'. In the late 1990s, the designer Kathy Formby, an American woman who had previously designed for Ralph Lauren, Calvin Klein and Tiffany & Co., launched the successful Two-in-One Circles and Squares bag, as well as the Three-in-One Frame bag, which had a removable suede clutch or shoulder bag to take you into the night.

T O D ' S
ONE MAN AND HIS MARKET

J P Tod (the original name of the brand) does not exist, but if he did he would be smart, preppy and WASPish. The name, the brand and the idea were a marketing dream thought out and researched by the Diego Della Valle Company of Italy. This company was set up by Dorino Della Valle, Diego's father, in the 1940s in the Ascoli Piceno region and was primarily concerned with shoe design. Some years ago it created new brands, including Tod's, Hogan and Fay – all of which have been successful, but especially Tod's. The rubber-studded driving shoe became a classic worn by the well-to-do and the fashion cognoscenti the world over. Despite the increasingly difficult economy in Italy, the group performed extraordinarily well, with the Tod's brand leading the way. Professor Michael Porter of the Harvard Business School used the company as an example of corporate excellence. Naturally, handbags, belts and small accessories were to follow. International recognition was achieved in the first year the Tod's handbag collection was launched.

The simple tote decorated with studs (*see right*) became a popular choice but their signature piece is the D-Bag, named for the late Diana, Princess of Wales. Diego Della Valle has said that the company chose to name the bag after Diana because 'She was an incredible supporter of our product'. Roomy, understated and with rolled handles, it has also been worn by Catherine, Duchess of Cornwall, as well as many Hollywood actresses.

TOP LEFT: **ACTRESS SARAH JESSICA PARKER**

VERSACE
ROCK STARS AND ROYALTY

Gianni Versace will always be remembered for bringing Hollywood glamour back to the catwalk and creating dresses that could launch careers, like that of Elizabeth Hurley. Born in southern Italy, which was known in antiquity as 'Greater Greece', Gianni chose the head of the mythical figure Medusa to be his company's logo because it represented 'the beauty and almost fatal fascination of the classical Greek tradition'. But the logo went on to represent the glamour and hedonism of the rock 'n' roll lifestyle Versace customers aspired to. His Medusa bag with studs, from his autumn/winter 1992–3 collection, was carried by Madonna and Sharon Stone, and his Marilyn print bag, with handles made from costume jewellery, found favour with supermodels and inevitably became a collectors' item. His friendship with Diana,

Princess of Wales, who attended his funeral in 1997, prompted the Lady Diana bag in 1995. He famously said he liked to dress egos and that those who did not have big egos could forget it.

The brand has since collaborated with H&M to release a collection that included blingtastic bags that are heavy on the hardware.

L O U I S   V U I T T O N
T R A V E L L I N G   R I G H T

Now that it is possible to circumnavigate the world in not much more than a day, appreciating the implications of travelling 150 years ago is difficult to do. In 1852 when Napoleon became Emperor, France was blossoming and opulence had come into fashion. The full gowns women wore had to be carefully packed and laid away when they travelled, and master trunk-makers were commissioned to design custom-built pieces for just that purpose. It was to one of these men that a young Louis Vuitton apprenticed himself, and in 1853 the 33-year-old Louis became the Empress Eugenie's favourite. A year later he opened his own shop. He quickly began to design his own canvases, but his striped and chequerboard patterns were soon imitated, so in 1896 he stopped using geometric lines and came up with the four-point star that is used today.

Despite the vagaries of fashion, Louis Vuitton adapted his trunks and suitcases to suit the age of the transatlantic steamers, the great rail journeys and the advent of aeroplanes, and they remain the *sine qua non* of luggage for the sophisticated traveller. To celebrate 150 years, the company asked several fashion designers to create their own bag, with surprising results, such as Vivienne Westwood's bum bag (*see page 156*), Romeo Gigli's amphora bag and Helmut Lang's dinner-jacket case. Other collaborations evolved with Stephen Sprouse, Rei Kawakubo, Sophia Coppola and, in 2003, Takashi Murakami and Marc Jacobs who created the multicolour monogram. The Damier Graphic, their classic check but in black and grey, was released in 2008.

ALEXANDER**WANG**
DOWNTOWN STYLE

Alexander Wang is every fashion-conscious girl's go-to brand for cool-without-trying handbags. The New York-based designer launched his eponymous line in 2004 aged just 19 and quickly established a loyal following with his grunge-chic style sensibility and cutting-edge bags.

Fittingly, the inspirations for Wang's designs are just as down-to-earth and street. 'Most of the time, it's on my walk to work, or sitting in the subway and seeing something random or out of context,' he has said. 'I'm not like most designers, who have to set sail on an exotic getaway to get inspired.'

Nevertheless, Wang still puts a lot of effort into his handbags with perhaps the label's most famous design, the Coco duffel, generating excitement even before its catwalk debut in 2009. A classic example of tough glamour, the Coco takes no prisoners with its hard-hitting edgy style. Textured black leather pulled tight around a boxy shape and – in a classic piece of Wang showmanship – a base entirely covered in gold studs. The result is an eye-catching blend of innovation, daring and versatility.

Ever since the Coco, the designer has delivered a series of bold design classics with shapes and finishing touches that always seek to surprise, such as the Brenda Zip Chain and the Darla Pyramid – a funky triangular clutch of particular note. Whether or not you feel brave enough to pull one off, one thing is indisputable – an Alexander Wang bag will add attitude to even the tamest outfit.

OPPOSITE AND RIGHT **THE JADE STING RAY CLUTCH AND THE RYAN TOTE BOTH FEATURE PRISTINE WHITE LEATHER AND ROSE-GOLD HARDWARE**

VIVIENNE WESTWOOD
COSTUME DRAMA

Vivienne Westwood knows no fear. In the clothes she designs and in her personal life she has done everything her own way, sometimes shocking but always enthralling both adoring fans and 'tut-tutting' onlookers. Westwood's first shop in the King's Road, London, sold 1950s-inspired clothes and memorabilia when the rest of the world was enjoying a hippie love-in. By 1974 she had moved on to clothing influenced by sadomasochism and the shop name was changed to Sex. She and her partner, the late Malcolm McLaren, were prosecuted under the obscenity laws, but that only seemed to encourage them and together they pioneered the anarchic Punk movement. When their relationship and design collaboration ended in 1983, Westwood proceeded to wow the fashion world with her mini 'Crini' collection, paired with skyscraper platform shoes. By 1987 her re-worked eighteenth-century corsets were 'must-haves'. Her love affair with the art and fashion of the past is evident in all her collections, but is translated with a new perspective. At the 1998 launch of her first perfume, Boudoir, Westwood presented the journalists with a mini Gladstone-style handbag made in a pink toile de Jouy canvas and trimmed in gold leather. The bag epitomized her highly feminine ideals and designs. Wherever – in terms of time and place – her inspiration comes from, her orb motif always identifies her work.

ADDRESS BOOK

Aigner
www.etienneaigner.com

Bill Amberg
www.billamberg.com

Balenciaga
www.balenciaga.co.uk

Barbour
www.barbour.com

Bottega Veneta
www.bottegaveneta.com

Tory Burch
www.toryburch.com

Cartier
www.cartier.co.uk

Chanel
www.chanel.com

Hervé Chapelier
www.hervechapelier.com

Chloé
www.chloe.com

Coach
uk.coach.com

Connolly
www.connollylondon.com

J & M Davidson
www.jandmdavidson.com

Dior
www.dior.com

Carlos Falchi
www.carlosfalchi.com

Fendi
www.fendi.com

Fenwick
www.fenwick.co.uk

Ferragamo
www.ferragamo.com

Gucci
www.gucci.com

Lulu Guinness
www.luluguinness.com

Nathalie Hambro
www.hanbro-art.com

Harrods
www.harrods.com

Harvey Nichols
www.harveynichols.com

Hermès
www.hermes.com

Anya Hindmarch
www.anyahindmarch.com

Marc Jacobs
www.marcjacobs.com

Donna Karan
www.donnakaran.com

Orla Kiely
www.orlakiely.com

Calvin Klein
www.calvinklein.com

Michael Kors
www.michaelkors.com

Launer
www.launer.com

Judith Leiber
www.judithleiber.com

Liberty
www.liberty.co.uk

Loewe
www.loewe.es

Longchamp
www.longchamp.com

Alexander McQueen
www.alexandermcqueen.
com

Mulberry
www.mulberry.com

Osprey
www.ospreylondon.com

Prada
www.prada.com

Yves Saint Laurent
www.yvessaintlaurent.co.uk

Selfridges
www.selfridges.com

Kate Spade
www.katespade.com

Pauric Sweeney
www.pauricsweeney.com

Tanner Krolle
www.tannerkrolle.com

Tod's
www.tods.com

Versace
www.versace.com

Louis Vuitton
www.louisvuitton.com

Alexander Wang
www.alexanderwang.com

Vivienne Westwood
www.viviennewestwood.co.
uk

INDEX

ACKNOWLEDGEMENTS

160

The publishers would like to thank the following sources for their kind permission to reproduce the pictures in this book:

The Advertising Archives: 17br, 19, 23, 80t, 91b, 95br, 95tl, 96, 150, 152-153
Aigner: 64
Anya Hindmarch: 110-111
Barbour & Sons: 25bl, 50br, 73
Bill Amberg: 65
Calvin Klein: 116-117
Camera Press: /Simon Archer: 129, /Stephane Benito 38tr, / Jacques Giaume: 128, Jerome Laurent: 67, Pierre Mandereau: 68, /Richard Open 40, /Anthea Simms: 155
Carlos Falchi: 92, 93
Carlton Books/Patrice de Villiers: 1, 2-3, 4-5 (Thierry Mugler), 7 (Lulu Guinness), 8 (Angela Hale collection), 9 (Anya Hindmarch, Kate Spade), 44-45 (Gucci), 51, 54t, 55-59, 60-61, 94, 108t, 121b, 140-141, 158
Cartier: 52tl, 74-75
Céline, Paris: 50tl, 76-77
Chanel: 29bl, 80bl, 80br, /Alvaro Canovas: 78bl, /Stephane Ciceron 52tr, 78t, /Laurent Herail: 79b, /Karl Lagerfeld: 81
Coach: 86-87
Condé Nast Publications: /Paul Bowden: 98bl, 114-115, / Coopers: 156t, /Clive Corless: 98bc, /Arthur Elgort: 10, 46, /Robert Erdmann: 62, /Olberto Gili: 137tr, /Andrew Lamb: 134br, 135, 136l, / Mark Liddell: 136r, /Raymond Meier: 136b, /Sid Pithwa: 136l, /Rapid Eye: 156b, /Claus Wickrath 26l

Connolly: 88-89
Christian Dior Couture: 90t, 90b, 91t
Christopher Moore: 26r, 28, 29r, 100l, 148r, 149l
Corbis: /Bettmann: 36tr, 39
Getty Images: 16, 17t, 18, 20, 21, 30, 37tl, 43, 66, 69l, 69r, 71, 85, 106, /The Image Gate: 70, 72, 154, /Gamma-Rapho: 85bl, 118r, 119, 133, 134l, /Wirelmage: 84, 112, 118l
Gucci: /Raymond Meier: 98br, 100b, 101, /Mario Testino: 99
Hermès: /Frederic Dumas 41c, 107, 108b
Hervé Chapelier: 53, 82-83
J P Tod's: 50bl, 146-147
Jason Bell: 95tr
Judith Leiber: 53b, 122, 123r, 124-125,
Justin Downing: 136b
Kobal Collection: 16br, 24, 35
Launer: 120, 122b
Loewe: 126
London Features International: 36bl, /Phil Loftus: 48, /Denise Van Tine 27br
Longchamp: 127
Louis Vuitton, Malletier A Paris: 14tl, 31, 151, 152
Lulu Guinness: 52l, 102-103
Marc Jacobs: 113
Mirror Syndication International: 79t
Mulberry: 34, 54bl, 130-131
Mary Evans Picture Library: 12, 13tl, 15, /Bruce Castle Museum: 14br /Fawcett Library: 13
Osprey: 132
Pauric Sweeney: /Declan Hogan: 142-143
Pictorial Press: 25br, /Zuma Miller: 42tr
Press Association Images: 37br, 38bl, 49, /Neil Munns 32

Salvatore Ferragamo: 97
Sotheby's Press Office: 104
Retna Pictures: /Steve Chys: 123l, /Bill Davila: 42l, 108r, / Steve Granitz: 41r, 27l, /King Collection: 22, /Larry Lazlo: 42br,
Rex Features: /Sipa Press: 105
The Ronald Grant Archive: 24br
Tanner Krolle: 50r, 144-145,
Telegraph Colour Library: / Benelux Press: 160
Topham Picturepoint: 41bl
Versace: 148b, 149t, 149b
Vivienne Westwood: 157
Yves Saint Laurent: 139, /Rive Gauche: 138

Every effort has been made to acknowledge correctly and contact the source and/or copyright holder of each picture, and Carlton Books Limited apologizes for any unintentional errors or omissions, which will be corrected in future editions of this book.

Special thanks are due to Deborah Fioravanti, Gianluigi Parenti at Prada (London), Caroline Kemp at Time Products PLC, Paula Snow at Connolly, and everyone who kindly supplied images for this book.

I am indebted to all the companies mentioned in this book whose wonderful PR directors have kindly provided valuable information and visuals. Thanks also to those who have helped me along the way, in particular Katie Sharer, Martha Delap and especially Dominic Drew. For the historical part of the text I must credit and thank Enid Nemy for her informative words in the book *Judith Leiber: The Artful Handbag*, the Victoria & Albert Museum for its wonderful collection, and Bill Amberg for his insight. I am also grateful to Venetia Penfold for asking me to write this book and to Alexandra Shulman, my editor at *Vogue*, for allowing me to do so.

Carmel Allen